The Poetry of Rudyard Kipling

The Poetry of Rudyard Kipling

Rousing the Nation

ANN PARRY

OPEN UNIVERSITY PRESS
Buckingham · Philadelphia

Open University Press
Celtic Court
22 Ballmoor
Buckingham
MK18 1XW

and
1900 Frost Road, Suite 101
Bristol, PA 19007, USA

First Published 1992

A catalogue record of this book is available from the British Library

Library of Congress Cataloging-in-Publication Data

Parry, Ann, 1949–
The poetry of Rudyard Kipling : rousing the nation / by Ann Parry.
p. cm.
Includes bibliographical references and index.
ISBN 0–335–09495–3 (hb)–ISBN 0–335–09494–5 (pb)
1. Kipling, Rudyard, 1865–1936–Poetic works. 2. Political poetry, English–History and criticism. I. Title.
PR4858.P58P37 1992
821′.8–dc20 91–46582
CIP

Typeset by Colset Private Limited, Singapore
Printed in Great Britain by St Edmundsbury Press Limited
Bury St Edmunds, Suffolk

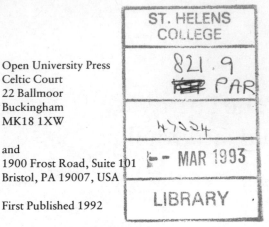

In memory of my parents

Contents

Acknowledgements

All deficiencies are of course my own, but I owe a debt of thanks to the following: Ray Jenkins, Owen Ashton, Rhys Garnett, Sandra Kemp, John Briggs, George Webb, Lisa Lewis, Derek Longhurst, Margaret Delaney, Cedric Parry and the late Syd Rowe.

Introduction

> Rudyard Kipling's history as a writer illustrates one of the most serious problems in modern criticism, the relationship between members of the Establishment [in both England and the United States] and writers who, for one reason or another, do not seem to satisfy the Establishment's expectations of what they *should* be saying and writing.[1*]

At a time when poetry had ceased to be the dominant literary mode, Rudyard Kipling was a popular poet. By 1918, large numbers of all his major collections had been printed: 81,000 of *Departmental Ditties*, 182,000 of *Barrack-Room Ballads*, 132,000 of the *Seven Seas* and 110,000 of the *Five Nations*. By 1931, when his stock was low with the literary establishment, these numbers had still risen significantly: *Barrack-Room Ballads* then recorded 255,000, *Departmental Ditties* 117,000, *Seven Seas* 187,000 and *Five Nations* 145,000. The volume, *The Years Between*, that contained poetry written during the First World War had sold 95,000. *The Definitive Edition* of Kipling's verse appeared in 1940 and has never been out of print; by April 1982, there had been 60 impressions of it. Despite this remarkable publishing history, no sustained attention from literary critics has been devoted to Britain's last popular political poet, the first in an age of democratic reform.[2] Moreover, since the collections of verse published during Kipling's lifetime were subsumed within the *Inclusive Editions*, which were used by the author from 1919 onwards to portray his overview of

*Superscript numerals refer to numbered notes at the end of the book.

British history, the original contexts have been elided and it is difficult for the reader to follow developments, varying intentions and changes of attitudes in the verses.[3]

The skirmishing that surrounded Kipling's reputation during his lifetime is well known. In 1899, W.T. Stead had praised him as the interpreter of the popular consciousness and the inspiration for the popular imagination, while others, such as Buchanan and Spencer, attacked him for abetting the recrudescence of barbaric ambitions and sentiments.[4] Then, as now, Kipling's fiction attracted most critical attention, and modern commentators who have interested themselves in his poetry have 'perpetually debated' the question: 'Is Kipling a poet?' T.R. Henn's answer to this question is not untypical: when his technical mastery, variety and craftsmanship have all been recognized, it has to be said that 'Kipling, nearly, but never wholly achieved greatness . . . the ultimate depth was lacking', because there was 'an absence of that highbreeding which is the essence of all style'.[5]

The values of high literature, 'greatness', 'style', 'highbreeding' and 'ultimate depth', which are lacking in Kipling, and therefore relegate him to the second rank, also define the popular of which he is a representative. Kipling's poetry is seen as a failure to be something else, it is lacking in the range of qualities and characteristics for which high literature is valued. This definition of literature depends greatly upon the ephemerality of popular texts: they must be lacking in aesthetic complexity because they disappear so quickly. It is at this point that Kipling becomes an enigma, because his popularity has never receded. In 1982, Kipling's books were 'selling at the rate of approximately 250,000 copies a year, more in the United Kingdom than in the United States, of course, but the record of sales – taken together – is fairly creditable for an author now almost half a century dead and buried'.[6] Two major publishers are in the process of reprinting his prose work with new introductions.[7] However, continuing demand for a writer's work long after his death is one of the criteria that suggests literary greatness and value, and this perhaps explains why there are a group of critics who have sought to admit Kipling to the first rank of literature, having duly chastised him for harmful attitudes, or having qualified his moral undesirability.

The sales of Kipling's work and the vagaries of his reputation indicates, as Gramsci suggested, that the popular is not to be thought of as something requiring definition. Rather, it is something that is constantly being reformed in the continuous and uneven struggles through which the dominant culture seeks to confine the popular. In such an environment, poetry does not carry its meaning inscribed on it forever. The uses to which it has been and will be put depend upon the ways in which it is articulated within a whole network of ideological relations at any particular historical conjuncture. The present work starts from the assumption that the effectiveness of political poetry depends upon its availability for different readings at different social levels. To use the terms of contemporary literary theory, the signifier is over-determined and moveable, it is permanently available for new uses:

> . . . one only has to listen to poetry . . . for a polyphony to be heard, for it to become clear that all discourse is aligned along the several staves of a score. There is in effect no signifying chain that does not have, as if attached to punctuation of each of its units, a whole articulation of relevant contexts suspended 'vertically' . . . from that point.[8]

The relationships observable within the signifying chains of poetry, as they are 'fitted' more or less successfully into the status quo of the cultural and literary experiences of various social groups and circles of readers, provide a guide both to Kipling's own reader hypotheses and the ways in which these did or did not relate to readers outside the text. The object of study of this book, therefore is not just poems by Kipling, but the reading formations which concretely and historically organize the practice of reading, 'connecting texts and readers in specific relations to one another . . . constituting readers as reading subjects of particular types, and texts as objects-to-be-read in particular ways'.[9] Such an examination reveals the areas of exchange in these years between different reading publics and opposing class cultures.

The book is arranged in six chapters, the first discusses *Early Verse* and *Departmental Ditties & Other Verses* in their Anglo-Indian and metropolitan contexts. The second is concerned with *Barrack-Room Ballads & Other Verses*, the volume with which Kipling established himself as the voice of the Empire. The third chapter deals with *The Seven Seas*, in which he set out his hopes for imperial federation. The fourth continues with a consideration of *The Five Nations*, essentially a response to the Boer War and what this was seen to have revealed about Britain and what it portended for the Empire. Chapter 5, which focuses on *The Years Between*, looks at Kipling's involvement with the Radical Right and the verses he wrote about the First World War. Throughout there is consideration of the reception of Kipling's verse by reviewers and the literary relations this produced. The final chapter assesses the ways in which criticism has modified and moved Kipling's poetry about in different ways – to locate it within different reading formations, reproducing it as different texts for different readers in accordance with shifting and variable literary and political objectives. All page references given are to the poems as they appear in the *Definitive Edition of Rudyard Kipling's Verse* published by Hodder and Stoughton.

ONE

'Official Sinning'

Early Verse 1879–89
Departmental Ditties & Other Verses 1886–90

When, in 1941, T.S. Eliot compiled what is still today the most widely known anthology of Kipling's verse, he chose not to include any material from the author's first collection. It was, he said, merely 'light reading in an English newspaper in India'.[1] Throughout its early life, although *Departmental Ditties & Other Verses* proved popular with many readers, reviewers responded to it more ambiguously. They either misrepresented it by over-emphasizing a few poems of a certain type, or they dismissed it altogether. T.S. Eliot clearly aligned with this latter group, although, in 1941, with decolonization under way in India, it was perhaps not surprising that the verse should be represented as the local ephemera of a bygone age. Fifty years later, colonial discourse is the focus of much attention from critics, theorists and historians alike, yet none of it has concentrated on the kind of imperial discourse that Kipling produced while he was a journalist in India.[2] The passage of *Departmental Ditties & Other Verses*, however, through a variety of reading formations, first in India and then in England, only in the end to be consigned to its place of origin as a type without merit, just when Anglo-India was on the brink of dissolution, suggests that its history might throw some light on the national identities offered to the English during this period, as well as providing insight into the relationship between the metropolitan and the periphery.

Departmental Ditties & Other Verses are only known today in the form in which they appear in the *Definitive Edition of Kipling's Verse.*[3] This grouping of the poems is based upon the fourth edition, prepared by Kipling shortly after he arrived in this country from India in 1889. The collection is prefaced by the 'Prelude', which was written especially for the English edition and its effect was, and is, to obscure the previous constitution and inscription of the verses in relation to their first Anglo-Indian audiences. Worse still, the effect is compounded in the *Definitive Edition* by the date 1885 being attached to the 'Prelude', which makes it appear that all the poems that follow were, although written in India, nevertheless produced with an English audience in mind. However, the original *Ditties* were only ten in number, and were published in a short period in 1886, between 5 February and 13 April, in the *Civil & Military Gazette* of Lahore.

This newspaper 'served a local community of about seventy Europeans, not counting military personnel. So small a group could provide an occasional social note, scandal or crime, but local news could come nowhere near filling the eighteen pages published daily.'[4] World and Indian news, gleaned from Reuter's, would fill another column or so, but the rest of the copy came from the ingenuity of the editors, of whom Kipling was the 'sub'. Most of the poems that will be discussed in this chapter were, like *Plain Tales from the Hills*, written to fill the remaining space in the day's copy of either the *Civil & Military Gazette* or the *Pioneer* of Allahabad.

The ten original *Ditties*, which appeared at weekly intervals, barely acknowledged the existence of native India. They were solely concerned with such day-to-day preoccupations of Anglo-Indians as pay, promotion and the vagaries of government departments. In this journalistic context, alongside other items either of a newsworthy or literary nature, clearly one of their intentions was to raise a smile, to be 'merry as the custom of our caste'.[5] There was, as Edward Farley Oaten noted in his essay on Anglo-Indian literature, a long tradition of light verse of this kind, 'what he [Kipling] had done in the ditties, many a predecessor had accomplished albeit a little less cleverly'. His additional comment that '*Departmental Ditties* . . . are little more than topical', was both a key to and, at the same time, an underestimation of the effect they had on one part of the Anglo-Indian community.[6] Many of the incidents recounted in the original *Ditties* were farcical, like the story of the young man in 'Pink Dominoes', who went to a masked ball 'to sit in the dusk and spoon', kissed the wrong girl, who just happened to be the young wife of 'Sir Julian Vouse, / Our big Political gun', who was persuaded to make the youngster his secretary.[7] All of the verses featured members of government departments, possibly real figures, who indulged in 'official sinning'.[8]

Immediately, the short series of poems found an appreciative audience among some groups in the Raj, 'Men in the Army, and the civil service, and the railway, wrote to me saying that the rhymes might be made into a book'.[9] They passed into wider circulation because their rhythms leant themselves easily to popular musical tunes, 'Some of them had been sung to the banjoes around camp fires, and some had run as far down the coast as Rangoon and Moulmein, and up to Mandalay'.[10] These particular characteristics of Kipling's writing, its topicality, the ready entrance it found into non-literary circles, and the ease with which it integrated into existing popular forms of entertainment, in this case the camp-fire sing-song, were to persist throughout his career and are part of the reason his verse played such a significant role in constructing a narrative of nationhood.

The enthusiastic reception that the *Ditties* had achieved as newspaper ephemera encouraged Kipling to risk becoming his own publisher, and the title of the book emerged from the form of the first edition. Paying for the use of the newspaper plant and working after office hours, the author produced:

> . . . a sort of book, a lean oblong docket, wire-stitched, to imitate a D. O Government envelope printed on one side only, bound in brown paper, and secure with red tape. It was addressed to all heads of departments and all government officials, and among a pile of papers would have deceived a clerk of twenty years service.[11]

The new apparel of the *Ditties* was an eye-catching, impudent way of reappearing before its colonial audience, and it gave the work a further dimension. The verse now maintained the pretence of having been produced from within the actual machinery of government. What had been occasional newspaper ephemera surrounded by various items of the same type, took on the appearance of an official, government-sanctioned report on its subject. It was as if the government had become, (as was indicated in 'The Last Department'), 'the subject matter of [its] own Report', an object for investigation.[12] Taken from their journalistic context in which they had appeared as passing jokes, quickly forgotten, they had grown into a collection, a more endurable form, and they offered, with official sanction it seemed, an extended comment on the governors of the Raj. Such a concentration on the Indian Civil Service and its members occurred at a peculiar moment in its history.

By the late nineteenth century, the Indian Civil Service symbolized more than anything else the power of England in India. However, to educated Indians who looked for advancement and found it closed to them, it represented the despotic presence of England. Since the Mutiny, the educated Indian, or Babu as he was scornfully known, had been perceived as a threat to British rule, especially if he were to gain entry to the Covenanted Civil Service by open competition in England.

A variety of means culminating in the Act of 1870 had been used to ensure that the majority of Covenanted posts were reserved for Englishmen. Indians were restricted to the judicial branch with lower rank and pay. Surendranath Banerjea had led protests in 1877 and 1878 against the reactionary policy of the government towards the new class of Indian and in 1883 the Indian National Conference at Calcutta took the decision to organize and fight the restrictions.[13]

This unrest in the periphery occurred simultaneously with an ongoing debate in the metropolitan about England's imperial role and her relationship with India. While Disraeli and the Conservatives were in power, between 1874 and 1880, Anglo-Indians felt some security, because, in aiming to restore Britain to what they considered to be its rightful place among the powers of Europe, India was indispensable. Disraeli's empire was, as one historian has put it, 'India oriented'.[14] When Cyprus was acquired, 'the movement', declared Disraeli, was 'not Mediterranean, it is Indian'.[15] Parallel with, and, of course, not unconnected with this conception of India's importance to England, was the assumption that, in the foreseeable future, the periphery must remain under English suzerainty, because, as Kipling had put it, in 1885, India was full of:

> Ill-conditioned peoples who
> Would fight
> At once like wolves if we withdrew
> Our right
> Of interference . . .[16]

Stated in this way, the conservative ideology of permanence, which Kipling had accepted, was able to clothe its involvement in India in the righteous garb of a civilizing mission that gave law and order to a barbaric country.

This view of the imperial relationship was contested by the Liberals and the Radicals. During the 1870s, in debates in widely read and respected journals, Gladstone in particular stridently refuted men like Edward Dicey, the Conservative editor of *The Observer*, who argued that England's power and greatness depended upon its imperial position. To protect her standing, Dicey argued that England should occupy Egypt which would then protect the route to India which was the keystone to the whole matter. He added that, 'to say we have been influenced in the main by any higher motive seems to me self-deception . . . to assert that we have gone forth to foreign lands for the sake of doing good would be sheer hypocrisy, we may fairly say that we have done good by going and are doing good by staying'.[17] Kipling too had adopted this kind of hard-headed morality in *Departmental Ditties* when, at the outset, he pointed to the less savoury imperial motives that had preceded its order-keeping, law-giving manifestations. The first of the 'race':

> Stole the steadiest canoe,
> Ate the quarry others slew,
> Died – and took the finest grave.[18]

Such a vision of England's imperial role was anathema to Gladstone and most Liberals. To them the Empire was a trust, a responsibility that England had to fulfil by passing onto it institutions that ensured freedom and voluntarism: 'The root and pith and substance of the material greatness of our nation lies within the compass of these islands, and is, except in trifling particulars, independent of all and every sort of political dominion beyond them'.[19] India, he believed, detracted from England's military strength and, rightly judged, this country should have 'no interest in India except the well-being of the land itself'.[20] However, neither the Liberals nor the Radicals called for the dissolution of the Empire, but they were minimalists: 'While we are opposed to imperialism', explained Gladstone, 'we are devoted to empire'.[21] Liberals wished to see no further imperial annexations and they looked – ideally though of course – in the future to a 'free association of largely independent colonies of British settlement held together by ties of friendship and affection'.[22] In his Midloathian campaign, in the election of 1880, which the Liberals won, Gladstone frequently reiterated this position on imperial issues and suggested that the Afghan War, precipitated by the Conservative Viceroy, Lord Lytton, had endangered the moral character and liberal traditions of England.

The appointment of the Marquis of Ripon, whose opinions were consonant with those of Gladstone, created alarm and unease in Anglo-India and some of Kipling's early verse articulated this fear in abrupt and unadorned terms. He prophesied in 'Trial by Judge' that:

> . . . in a few more decades, to
> United India we,
> With one consent, our Government
> Resign and homeward flee.[23]

The fear was exacerbated by the signs of unrest there already were among the native middle classes, who were looking for careers and a role in their own government that befitted their education. Ripon arrived determined to remove the impression from the minds of Indian people that they took second place to England's schemes in central Asia. To do so he tried to improve the position of the small class of highly educated natives. What had particularly annoyed this group was Salisbury's lowering of the age limits for the Indian Civil Service (ICS) competitive examinations. Ripon proposed, therefore, to raise the upper age limit to 21 and to give credit to those candidates competent in Arabic and Sanskrit, just as was given to Britons qualified in Latin and Greek. He never, it seems, regarded the ICS as anything other than an essentially British service, 'the backbone of the administration', but he did look to the satutory service, in an improved form, as the best channel for Indians to enter into senior official employment.[24] It was not his intention to swamp the civil service with Indians to an extent that would be unsafe – in no one year would the intake to both services amount to more than 18 per cent. However, he did believe that educated Indians possessed legitimate ambitions. They were no longer to be disregarded because they now understood their oppression and were developing skills to resist it. If they came to the conclusion that their representations to the Raj were ignored, then they might turn their attention to inciting the masses to opposition. Ripon did not wish this to happen, particularly while he was Viceroy; he wanted loyalty and support for British rule from educated Indians, not disaffection and enmity.

Such an outlook, not surprisingly, was antipathetic to many of those who held the highest posts in the ICS, which by the 1880s took comfort in the 'illusion of permanence' that was consonant with conservative imperial ideology.[25] This permanence was, as we have seen, justified by considerations of strategy, power, profit and a civilizing mission. By the second half of the nineteenth century, the reformist enthusiasm associated with Bentinck and Macaulay had long since ebbed. The Mutiny of 1857 was used to justify attitudes that existed before, so that the aim of the government of India became, as 'The Masque of Plenty' showed, to produce 'The Much Administered Man', rather than to transform Indians into mimicking white men. An enormous amount of energy was devoted to administrative efficiency. The policies of the 1870s, 1880s and 1890s were strongly influenced by the thinking of men like John Strachey and James Fitzjames Stephen, who took the Hobbesian view that people needed strong government and security rather than freedom. Moreover, what the British perceived to be India's barbarism and heathenism required and rationalized their autocratic presence. Fitzjames Stephen stressed the need for administrative order above everything else. In 1883, he wrote in this way about the 'Foundations of the Government of India':

> Now the essential parts of European civilization are peace, order, the supremacy of the law, the prevention of crime, the redress of wrong, the enforcement of contracts, the development and

> concentration of the military force of the state, the constitution of public works, the collection and expenditure of revenue required for these objects in such a way as to promote to the utmost the public interest, interfering as little as possible with the comfort, or wealth of the inhabitants, and the improvement of the people.[26]

When England's role in India was conceived in terms of the autocratic dispensation of administrative efficiency there was no possibility of any meeting point between Anglo-Indian and native cultures. The gap between ruler and ruled was absolute and after the Mutiny it was clearly recognized that, fundamentally, British rule was secured by and dependent upon a military presence. In 1876, when he was Secretary of State for India, Salisbury reminded Disraeli of 'the nakedness of the sword on which we relied'.[27] The adventures of *Soldiers Three* on active service made the same point, and, significantly Dufferin's repeated advice to Lansdowne in 'One Viceroy Resigns' was that, whenever money was unexpectedly available it should be used on 'Guns always – quietly – but always guns.'[28]

The growth, therefore, of an articulate and politically self-conscious native middle class, although treated in terms of contempt and derision by many Anglo-Indians was, at the same time, realized as a potential threat to the permanence of the Raj and its administrators. Since his arrival, no-one more than Kipling had ridiculed the aspirations of the Indians towards a say in government. In 'The Indian Delegates', written in 1885, on the occasion of a group travelling to England to try to persuade the electorate there of the justness of their cause, Kipling had written in the *Civil & Military Gazette*:

> The facts are simply thus,
> They are not homogenus;
> And Babus and Pathans will never mix;
> And the ryots when they rest,
> Do not study with a zest
> The course of Indo-British politics . . .[29]

The confrontation between Ripon's liberalism and the entrenched conservatism of the ICS came to a head over the Ilbert Bill, which would have allowed Indians to hear and pass judgment in cases against British subjects. Opposition from the expatriate community was extreme at what was seen as an erosion of British hegemony. The verses that Kipling wrote on 29 March 1883 showed the typical racist contempt of the community for native aspirations. They indicate the phobic racism that is an attempt to handle personal inadequacy which seemed to take its origins 'in ideologies of class, rather than in those of nation'.[30] The supposed animalism of the Indians degraded the breeding of the whites and inverted the 'natural' social hierarchy:

> But the Baboos that browsed in each office
> Of subordinate Civil Employ
> Cried Hurrah for our Viceregal novice!
> Hurrah for the Brahminee boy!
> Let the 'mean white' be silent, and doff his
> Pith hat to the Brahminee boy![31]

Quite clearly, natives who undermined the distinction between themselves and Europeans were intolerable. The 'Baboo' or 'the graduate of culture' had no claim to 'equality beside the higher race', because 'Though you paint him as a peacock, still the vulture is a vulture'.[32] The opposition of Anglo-India to the Ilbert Bill was, as these lines indicate, intense and hysterical and Ripon was forced to withdraw it. He resigned before the end of his tenure, to be replaced by Lord Dufferin, a Whig Unionist, whose arrival in India in December 1884 was barely noticed because it coincided with native demonstrations of support for Ripon as he departed the country. Kipling fired one last salvo at Ripon with his poem 'A Lost Leader', in which he declared that those who lived by 'words' were not men at all, because '*MEN* live by the work of their head and hand', and judged by these criteria Ripon had given India nothing.[33]

The new Viceroy, Lord Dufferin, soon let it be known that he also was disposed to pursue a liberal policy: he wished to support 'the beneficient projects' that Ripon had instituted for the good of the people.[34] However, while Anglo-India awaited with curious, even nervous expectation, to see in what particular constitutional directions these intentions would lead him, Dufferin had to depart Calcutta, ironically, to pursue a very illiberal imperial aim. He went to Mandalay, at first to assess the situation in Upper Burma, and later to oversee its annexation.[35] The affair of King Thibaw absorbed the whole of Dufferin's first year in India, but the aspirations of the native middle classes remained to the fore. In December 1885, the Indian National Congress met for the first time, and Anglo-India did not fail to note that, in this same month, Gladstone's conversion to Home Rule for Ireland became known. W.C. Bonnerjee, who presided over the meeting of the Congress, informed the assembled delegates that Dufferin had suggested that it should 'point out to the government in what respects the administration was defective and how it could be improved'.[36] Historians have suggested that the intention behind this request was to turn the Indian National Congress into a body that would perform the functions of Her Majesty's Opposition at home and 'counterbalance the conservative Anglo-Indians'.[37] This move was not, as might be imagined, greeted with enthusiasm by the administrators and governors of India.

It was in the context of these changes in India, and before Dufferin returned from Mandalay to give these constitutional matters his full attention, that *Departmental Ditties* began to be published. Their popularity took them as far as Mandalay and they were still appearing in March 1886, when he returned and began to consider the demands of the Indian nationalist organizations. The re-issue of the verses in the guise of a government report coincided with demonstrations by Indian associations to further their claims on the government. It was unlikely to say the least that the upper echelons of Anglo-Indian society, particularly the more conservative ones, would have regarded this as the most propitious moment to reveal, even in a light-heartedly satirical way, that those importantly involved in the government of India were essentially self-seeking, ambitious and immoral. In the peculiarly tense atmosphere that existed at this time, when some felt that the Anglo-Indian community was on the defensive, many had no wish to appear ridiculous before a new leader who was soon to take a hand in their fate. Least of all were they inclined to accept criticism from one 'Whose mode of earning money was a low and shameful one', who 'wrote for divers papers, which as everybody knows, / Is worse than serving in a shop or scaring off the crows'.[38]

Moreover, Dufferin's reputation as a respected imperial administrator did not suggest that it would be wise to begin a relationship with him by showing the classic bureaucratic characteristics of in-fighting, favouritism and corruption. He was a man who 'disliked yet did not try to understand the petty self-seeking and the ungentlemanly behaviour of the English official and mercantile middle class abroad, many of whom he encountered seeking title or wealth, or both, through influence and devious means that were odious to his aristocratic code of values'.[39] Dufferin was unlikely, therefore, to admire such figures as Delilah Aberystwyth, Ahaseurus Jenkins or Potiphar Gubbins, who inhabited the *Ditties*; indeed, some would have thought them better not paraded at this point. One of the last poems in the series, 'The Man Who Could Write', in showing the petty response of inner circles to criticism, gestured towards exactly the kind of behaviour that Dufferin was known to deplore:

> Boanerges Blitzen . . . made his seniors squirm,
> Quoted office scandals, wrote the tactless truth –

only to find that 'promotion didn't come to him' and he

Languished in a district desolate and dry;
Watched the Local Government yearly pass him by;
Wondered where the hitch was; called it most unfair.

That was seven years ago – and he still is there.[40]

The revelation of such official spite cast a dubious light on the probity and the competence of the administration. Poems that pretended to be the reports of actual incidents, which might refer to real people, and which recounted tales about 'the Little Tin Gods', who made foolish decisions, or the 'Public Waste' of a most competent engineer, pensioned off because he did not fit in with the highly artificial society which was ruled by the close-knit 'Laws of the Family', such verse did not appear to be supportive or respectful of Anglo-Indian society.[41] Neither did it confirm its intrinsic superiority to the alien culture in whose midst it was. In this situation, the satiric potential of these humorous verses became actual and cut the ground from beneath Anglo-Indian and conservative justifications for despotic rule. The duplicity shown in the *Ditties* by the representatives of England made it difficult to claim this as solely a characteristic of Indian people.

Furthermore, there was another feature of the *Ditties* that made them seem inappropriate at this moment: they all drew attention to the peculiar circumstances of the Anglo-Indian community. The situations with which most of the poems dealt – adulterous liaisons or administrative nepotism – were all a function of an island of English people forced together in the midst of an Indian sea. The dedication with which the protaganists concentrated on keeping alive the memory of English life, with dinners, balls, hunting, narrow moralism and domesticity, was quite clearly the means by which Anglo-India confirmed its difference from the native communities, while at the same time re-enforcing its connection with the metropolitan. The effect of such behaviour was, inevitably, to create an unbridgeable gap between colonial and Indian people. The *Gazette*, Kipling's own paper, reviewed the first edition of the poems and unconsciously recognized this perhaps when it lamented the absence from the verses of the native people of India. These absent subjects, even though disarticulated, were, nevertheless, a sign of the racism of the Empire and the tensions of that particular moment in the nineteenth century. There was a sense in which the introversion of the poems justified the liberal intentions of Ripon and Dufferin. The isolation of Anglo-Indian society was based upon contempt for Indians and there were *Ditties* that showed only too clearly that this was an intended and integral part of government policy.

'What Happened', not written until 1888, but, even at that distance, added by Kipling to the series called *Departmental Ditties* rather than to the *Other Verses*, was clearly seen by its author as part of the report on the Government of India.[42] 'Hurree Chunder Mookerjee . . . Barrishter-at-Lar' was supposed to be a representative of the Babu class, for it was to the Law that the educated Indian turned on finding the civil service closed to him. Mookerjee's learning is shown to be only skin-deep, he is portrayed as having as his highest aim the desire 'to wear / Sabres by the bucketful, rifles by the pair'. In response to this claim, 'the Indian Government winked a wicked wink' and allowed him to carry arms, so that he would create the same desire among his fellow 'hairy gentlemen' – who, once armed, promptly slaughtered one another. To the final question 'What became of Mookerjee?', the reader is told:

> . . . Ask Mahommed Yar
> Prodding Siva's bull down the Bow Bazar,
> Speak to placid Nubbee Baksh – question land and sea –
> Ask the Indian Congress men – only don't ask me![43]

The final parallel between the native characters in the poem and the Indian National Congress revealed once more the contempt of both the government and the speaker for native aspirations and the institution through which they sought a legitimate outlet. Further, the policy that was actually being implemented against it – exploiting its factionalism and using that as evidence of the incapacity of Indians to govern themselves – seemed designed to exacerbate rather than calm relations between the two communities.

Essentially, therefore, in this context, the *Departmental Ditties* could be seen to reveal, often in a critical or satirical light, both the corruption and conservatism of the Government of India. The *Sind Gazette* found the verse comic and truthful and it emphasized their authenticity; they had, it said, 'the genuine ring'. *The Indian Daily News* went more directly to the point when it observed that it saw in the series 'the lampooning of weak and corrupt officialism'.[44] Verse of this kind would have clearly had the capacity both to offend innermost circles and create a wrong impression with the new Viceroy. Despite their comic element, at this particular moment, when decisions were about to be taken that might alter the position of the Anglo-Indian community, these verses seemed, even if unintentionally, to underwrite the liberal convictions about the need for change. Moreover, if such work went beyond India, its satirical edge could easily bring the government into disrepute and ridicule and fuel that side of the imperial debate that wished for a move towards semi-independence in parts of the Empire. *Departmental Ditties* might easily confirm the well-known prejudice that *Vanity Fair* articulated when it said that all there was to the upper reaches of Anglo-India was 'duty, red-tape, picnics and adultery'.[45] The revelations about 'the Little Tin-Gods' on the mountainside at Simla were more than capable of initiating new myths.[46]

Presented as a series, therefore, and in the form of a government report, the verses cast a light on Anglo-India, which, at such a critical moment, might have seemed to some people less than funny and possibly very damaging. The display in *Departmental Ditties* of the inner workings of the ultimate symbol of British power in India at this time was compromising – revealing a rampant nepotism, an adulterous atmosphere and an isolationism that bred insecurity and racism. In *British Social Life in India*, Kincaid indicated that the Government of India, the elite core of the ICS, was less than enthusiastic about these verses or *Plain Tales from the Hills*. In response to them he says: 'Simla remained cold. The fellow [Kipling] was clearly a bounder; his stories of life in the Hills were informed by the natural envy of a cad who had sought and been refused an entree into Simla society.' Whatever the personal animus behind the verse, it was clear that much of its subject matter was gathered by Kipling on his annual leave at Simla. Sir Francis Younghusband, who served at Simla on the staff of the Quarter-Master General, spoke of Kipling as being 'looked upon with great disfavour by staff officers as being bumptious and above his station'. Kincaid further noted that his memsahib grandmother always spoke of Kipling as 'a subversive pamphleteer given to criticising his betters'.[47] This impression that the collection was adversely received is also confirmed by the fact that after the volume, *Echoes*, which he wrote in collaboration with his sister, neither the *Calcutta Review* nor the *Asiatic Quarterly Review*, chief voices of Anglo-Indian culture, reviewed his books – even after his recognition in England as the greatest writer that the Raj had produced. Obviously, *Departmental Ditties* were at odds with the representation of itself that government circles wished to project. They drew attention to those weaknesses that Liberals, in particular, wished to reform and that Conservatives preferred not to acknowledge.

Beyond government circles, the verses did not encounter such hostility. In fact, they proved even more popular with the larger imperial community than they had been in their weekly appearances in the newspaper. Those outside the charmed circle of government no doubt enjoyed deriding and laughing at the elite group to which they would never gain entrance. Orders for the *Departmental Ditties* flowed in, and these 'false documents' were 'posted . . . up and down the empire from Aden to Singapore, and from Quetta to Colombo'.[48] The first edition included verses written prior to the *Ditties* and a few that had just appeared in the newspaper. It sold out within a few weeks of its publication in June 1886, and demand for a new one arose. *Other Verses* were added so that the format of the collection had changed again as it went into second and third editions under the imprint this time of Thacker & Spink of Calcutta. The additional verses, which included such poems as 'One Viceroy Resigns' and 'The Masque of Plenty', were equally frank and open to adverse misinterpretation by outsiders, as those in the original group of *Ditties*.[49]

In relation to its first audiences, therefore, Kipling's work had received, not for the last time, a decisively different response from different parts of the society in which it had been produced. Its popularity with larger numbers was bought at the expense of the offence given to the powerful minority that symbolized the authority and superiority of the British in India. After the numerous verses that Kipling had written which mouthed Anglo-Indian attitudes, *Departmental Ditties* indicated either a complete misjudgement of the moment or a growing awareness in the writer that the 'superior race' might need to amend its ways if it were to maintain the permanent position for which it, and the author of these verses, wished.

However, before *Departmental Ditties* was expanded into its second and third editions, it received in October 1886 its first notice in England from no lesser person than Andrew Lang in his famous monthly column 'At the Sign of the Ship' in *Longman's Magazine*.[50] He had been sent, possibly by Kipling's editor and friend, E. Kay Robinson, the edition of *Departmental Ditties* that looked like a government report. Lang identified in the work two different strands: the corruption of the English in India, but also their sacrifice of themselves in an alien land. The impression the review made was determined by his allowing the 'sacrificial' theme to dominate.

In the first place, Lang described the verses as 'quaint and amusing', but then seemed to notice the critique they contained of the Government of India. Quoting a passage from a 'General Summary' that paralleled the 'official sinning' of the British Government in India with 'a fraud of monstrous size / On King Pharaoh's swart civilians', he commented that 'The Radical should read *Departmental Ditties* and learn how gaily *Jobus et Cie* govern India'.[51] Emphasis began to fall, therefore, on the satire of the poems rather than on them as 'a special variety of Vers de societe'. The stages of this response in many ways echoed those that had occurred in Anglo-India, where they had been seen by some as a joke, as light entertainment, and by others as pointed criticism. The satiric aspect of the verses was understood by Lang to lend support to those, like the Radicals, who earlier in the century had cried 'Emancipate your colonies' and who, although they were now more moderate, were nevertheless critical of the imperial enterprise. Lang commented that, 'On the whole these are melancholy ditties. Jobs, and posts, and pensions, and the wives of their neighbours appear [if we trust the satirist] to be much coveted by her Majesty's Oriental Civil Servants.'[52]

It was ironic, of course, that Lang should associate Kipling with a Radical point of view, but clearly it was just this construction that Simla had feared, and which accounted for its cool response. The Raj, in terms of fundamental liberal principles, was opposed to the most traditional tenets of English freedom, which was based on constitutional government. One of their responses to the despotic presence of England in India was to insist upon the supremacy of the home government at all times and on all matters. Imperial despotism in India would then be subject to the influence of the balance of authority that characterized government at home. What Lang failed to notice in relating the verses to a radical outlook was that they were as little enamoured of the metropolitan rulers of India as they were of those who governed it on the spot.[53]

'Pagett MP', written in June 1886 for the *Pioneer*, just in time to be included with the first edition, and a year after the Conservatives had returned to power in England, was directed at the ignorance of the metropolitan about the periphery.[54] This had been much commented on in 1876, when Disraeli, in a speech defending the Queen's accession to the title Empress of India, spoke about the colonist who, on arrival, found 'nuggets' of gold, who 'fleeces a thousand flocks', and returned to Great Britain to live in rich retirement.[55] In exposing this kind of ignorance, 'Pagett MP' revealed also the political tensions that lay at the heart of the relationship between Anglo-India and England. It caricatured an MP who presumed to be able 'to study the East' in 4 months, so that he might then return Home as an expert able to formulate policy for India. Pagett, with his 'Asian solar myths', mouthed what Anglo-India saw to be the perniciously misleading 'truths', rife especially among Liberal groups in the metropolitan, that the English in India whined about their lives, when actually they were living as aristocrats with very little to do, waited on by myriads of servants, and cushioned by 'princely pay'. Since 1857, Anglo-Indians had often felt that their best interests were dangerously compromised by 'the fools like Pagett' who write about their 'Eastern trips . . . And . . . the travelled idiots who duly misgovern the land.'[56] Since many in the ICS assumed the necessity of a permanent Raj, the ultimate control of the Government of India by the English constitution was a matter of serious concern. It encouraged those democratic ideas in the native middle classes, by which they felt threatened and outraged. According to the voice that tells the story of Pagett MP, the only cure for those with such notions was that they got to know for themselves the land and their 'Aryan brothers', who they would then surely 'hammer[ed] . . . in an illiberal way'.[57] The barely veiled allusion in this final phrase left the reader in no doubt which political ideology was, in the speaker's opinion, responsible for such notions. While, therefore, the writer of these verses might have shown Anglo-India in an unattractive light, it was not with the intention of advancing liberal conceptions of India. Rather, the existence of a critique of the metropolitan *and* the periphery suggests anxiety about both.

Lang either failed to notice or preferred not to comment on the way in which the author had implicated the metropolitan in his representation of the 'Jewel in the Crown'. One might suspect the latter, given the conclusion of the review which sought to encourage in readers a feeling of satisfaction and pride in English character. The best wine in the collection, Lang said, had been saved by the poet for one of the last poems which was called 'In Springtime'.[58] Lang thought so highly of this piece that he quoted it in full, thereby placing a heavy emphasis upon it. It was a poem of a particular type with a long history in Anglo-Indian writing – the song of an exile, the main effect of which was to assert 'the positional superiority' of England and the English.[59] India the land of 'endless sunshine' was portrayed as a place of excess, with its 'blossom-burdened bough', it was too fecund. It was everything that England was not and it made the true Briton exiled there 'sick'. The blazing colours of the garden, the chattering of the squirrels and the screaming of the birds indicated a demented environment that in its wildness necessitated subjugation. England, as symbolized in the images of the 'furrow of the ploughshare . . . the fragrance of the loam', represented the security of all that was temperate and balanced. The yearning of the exile for this harmony confirmed that he was its true representative in India; the metropolitan emerged as the best of all possible places in the world and the speaker's endurance and service in India revealed his heroism and the courage and character of the island race. The 'Othering' of India, with the emphasis on its absolute difference and distance from England, confirmed the need if not for a permanent Raj, at least for its existence in the foreseeable future. Implicitly, it suggested that India, as yet, was by no means ready to govern itself. It could even seem that in such a threateningly exotic environment as the one shown 'In Springtime', the vagaries of those who made such a 'sacrifice' and lived with 'the knell of exile' in their ears, seemed excused and the despotism of English rule necessary.[60]

The first inscription of *Departmental Ditties* within the metropolitan literary institution, therefore, situated them within a discursive framework that was able to assimilate criticism of the Raj and justify it on the grounds of the extreme otherness of the sub-continent. Such an inscription was fundamentally conservative because the representation of

India as different from and inferior to England also implied the necessity for a permanent Raj. India became a place where nature was distorted, where 'the rose has lost its fragrance, and the *koil's* note is strange'. Set against this was the rural idyll that was England, where 'the gusts are booming, o'er the brown fields . . . And the hawk nests on the cliffside and the jackdaw in the hill'. The metropolitan, and by extension those exiles who yearned for it, were glorified. An English reader could find in this homesickness a badge of national heroism, a sign of his superiority and difference from other races. This review, and many of the others that will be discussed, are examples of the way, at this point in the century, the institutions of literature developed in association with the idea of English imperial destiny. Significantly, however, this location of the verse had been achieved by sleight of hand, by suggesting to readers that what was really worth their attention was the 'best wine' in a single poem at the end, that dissolved the critique of the periphery and over-rode observations about the metropolitan.[61]

In a more scholarly review written 2 years later, Lang's manoeuvres were intensified. By 1888, the collection was in its third edition and had grown in size. The critique of empire had become more pointed in some poems, and it was therefore more difficult to assimilate within a discourse whose purpose was to encourage national satisfaction and self-congratulation. This was clearly the purpose of Sir William Hunter, who wrote the review in September in *The Academy*, a well-respected journal. Hunter had been Head of the Statistical Section in the Indian Civil Service and had retired from his post in June 1888 at the age of 47.[62] As a member of Lord Dufferin's Council, he would have been fully aware of the adverse response in government circles to Kipling's verse. Nevertheless, he wrote a favourable review. This was very surprising, because he himself had been the subject of a squib by Kipling in the *Pioneer Mail* that ridiculed him for his sympathy towards the Indian National Congress. Hunter's response to this had been dismissive and superior. He had commented to Kipling that it was 'to be regretted that you devote to clever trifles of this sort talents which are capable of much better things'.[63] Three months after the favourable review in *The Academy*, though perhaps before it fell into Kipling's hands in India, the young poet again poked fun at Hunter in 'One Viceroy Resigns'. He was portrayed as someone with little better to do than write letters to *The Times* and the poem suggested that his role in Council had been an obstructive one. His *métier* had been to raise objections with the Viceroy by 'silky' voiced interventions of 'Bat my lahd'.[64] However, Hunter was an old friend of Kipling's parents and had been asked by the poet's mother to try to secure a passage into England for her son's work. What he wrote suggests that it was not primarily his feelings of friendship towards the poet that inspired the favourable review. His greatest concern was that the metropolitan should see India and the British in India in a particular way.

Hunter's method of trying to achieve this end was to recommend the verse as a comment on the superiority of the English race, thereby convincing readers that 'our countrymen and countrywomen in India are trained to do England's greatest work on earth'.[65] Led by such a review, a reader would be inclined to pay particular attention to verse such as 'A legend of the Foreign Office' that portrayed India as the reverse of all that was English. Kolazai, the Kingdom of the Rajah Rustum Beg, typifies the mysterious East, with degraded traditions and a debauched ruler, who, when thwarted:

> Doubled taxes, cesses, all; cleared away each new built *thana*;
> Turned the two-lakh Hospital into a superb *Zenana* . . .

The poem relates a half-hearted attempt at Europeanization, matched by a more massive regression to the old ways, as the rajah once more 'Clad himself in Eastern garb'. This was India the unknowable and unchangeable, corrupted by chronic sexual and moral degeneracy.[66]

To maintain the focus on 'the nobler Anglo-Indian' world of sacrifice and mission, however, Hunter, like Lang, found it necessary to ignore a great deal of the collection, which was dismissed as trivial '*vers de société*'. He recommended just a few 'serious poems', which could be classified in terms of type, and then related to a tradition.[67] This became the means by which he was able to specify connections between metropolitan colonial discourse and that of the periphery. The real value of the collection, it was suggested, lay in what linked it to the work of others who had written about India in a particular way:

> To Mr Kipling as to Sir Alfred Lyall in our own time, or to poor Leyden in the past, and indeed to every man of the true literary temperament who has had to spend his years in India, that country is still the 'sultry and sombre Noverca – the Land of regrets'.[68]

Once the verses were placed in this context, people in England were able to see the sacrifices made by the white man in India, which, of course, confirmed the superiority of the race, when it was faced by the most gruelling physical conditions and a totally alien, foreign society:

> Heat, solitude, anxiety, ill-health, the never-ending pain of separation from wife and child, these are not the experiences which make men amusing in after life. But these are stern teachers who

> have schooled one generation of Anglo-Indian administrators after another to go on quietly and resolutely, if not hopefully, with their appointed task.[69]

Because such a backward place as India existed, the selfless English had to suffer and die, thousands of miles from home, in attempting to bring to it good government. The Raj was a symbol of the way Britain shared its culture with subject races and helped to civilize them. For all his liberalism, Hunter saw no end to this process, it had and would go on for 'generations'. The sub-continent had become the arena in which, as 'The Galley Slave' showed, national character had been tested and shown to survive heroically:

> Was it storm? Our fathers faced it and a wilder never blew;
> Earth that waited for the wreckage watched the galley struggle through,
> Burning noon or choking midnight. Sickness, Sorrow, Parting, Death?
> Nay your babes would mock you had they time for idle breath.[70]

The galley was, of course, the Anglo-Indian ship of state, and if you had served there you could be certain that you 'have lived and toiled with men'.

A fundamental requirement of this discourse of character building was the isolation of the periphery from the centre. This was the condition in which the worth of the English national character was proven, as 'Christmas in India' showed:

> Oh the toil that knows no breaking! Oh the *heimweh*, ceaseless, aching!
> Oh the black dividing Sea and alien Plain!
>
> Hard her service, poor her payment – she in ancient, tattered raiment –
> India, she the grim Stepmother of our kind.[71]

By identifying these poems as the ones of true value in the collection, Hunter produced a colonial discourse whose portrait of the English was of the noblest kind. 'With fruitless years behind us and the hopeless years before us', it seemed undoubtedly true that such self-sacrifice was 'England's greatest work on earth'.[72] Once again, however, this had only been achieved by dismissing, even castigating, some verses and ignoring others. 'A General Summary', which had, of course, inspired Lang to identify in *Departmental Ditties* grist to the Radical mill, was peremptorily dealt with by Hunter. He commented acerbically, 'If this were Mr Kipling's highest flight his poems would scarcely have reached a third edition.'[73] He was probably discomforted by more than the 'flippancy and cynicism' of the lines. The poem had been written especially to preface the *Ditties* when they were gathered together to look like a government report and the first lines declared:

> We are very slightly changed
> From the semi-apes who ranged
> India's prehistoric clay[74]

As the first item of address to Anglo-Indians their being linked with prehensiles may have struck only some of them as a joke. The connection was hardly useful to a reviewer determined to claim national and racial superiority as the basis of his justification for the continuation of empire. It was the refusal of some of the verses to fit in with his presentation of empire that led to them being ignored.

'The Masque of Plenty', for example, deliberately went out of its way to expose the realities of England's imperial existence that were obscured by the ideologies of order and efficiency dominant in the periphery and symbolized by the ICS. Through the use of an elaborate Swinburnian parody, the Government of India was portrayed as cripplingly short-sighted. On the heights of Simla, a ridge on the Himalayas, where for 7 months during the hot season the whole decision-making apparatus of India was concentrated, the government saw only what it wanted to see. In these comfortable surroundings, cut off from the heat of the plains, it was able to feel assured 'that our people are unanimously dining', and to believe that the age-old enemies of the land had retreated: 'We have said of the Sickness – "Where is it?" – and of Death / It is far from our ken.' This confident recitative comes with the accompaniment of an 'electroplated harp', a forewarning that beneath it a baser truth lay.[75]

This truth was put into the mouths of 'orientals' who spoke from 'Nowhere in particular' and who were, therefore, it was clearly implied, ubiquitous. The burden of their message was direct:

> Our cattle reel beneath the yoke they bear
>
> The well is dry beneath the village tree
> The young wheat withers 'ere it reach a span.
> And belts of blinding sand show cruelly
> Where once the river ran.

Later, the same native group commented:

> God bless the squire
> And all his rich relations
> Who teach us poor people

We eat our proper rations –
In spite of inundations,
Malarial exhalations,
And casual starvations.[76]

The government may have achieved its highest aim of producing 'The Much Administered Man', but the reality of the native's life remained poverty and disease. The universality of these realities undermined the justification claimed by the ICS for its vast administrative machinery and, more importantly, it seemed to the speaker of the poem that it constituted a threat to British power. Order and efficiency there might have been, but the poem indicated that these things had very little to do with real improvements to the physical well-being of the people of India. The voice in the poem is clearly reminding the Raj that while empire gave power and privileges, it also brought responsibilities and the governors of India earned their social place by performing a genuine social service – not always evidently fulfilled from the distance and comfort of Simla.

In 'The Masque of Plenty', the Raj appeared merely as an organization of the misery that existed, not an amelioration of it. The observant might see in the eye of the native a 'foreknowledge of debt', even though he 'toils and may not stop; . . . Between a crop and a crop.'[77] There was the added suggestion, therefore, that the native paid dearly for the administration of his poverty; and his awareness of this state of affairs ought to have been a warning to the Government of India of the potential resistance there was to its rule. 'The Masque of Plenty' suggested that the essence of the English presence in India was obfuscation about the real problems that existed there. It pointed to an administration cut off from the people it governed both by distance and the comforts with which it surrounded itself. These conditions, the poem implied, had become sources of illusion, which could be the undoing of the British in India. Hunter's heroic Britons labouring in the killing heat, Kipling's own 'William the Conqueror', had given way to imperial administrators isolated and endangered by their own ignorance.[78] There was little here to encourage satisfaction in either the metropolitan or the periphery. The verse pointed to the need for England to set its imperial house in order. There was no space for self-congratulation. A change was required that began with the realization that England's hold on India was potentially tenuous. 'The Masque of Plenty' undercut those imperial discourses that encouraged the 'sun-ward gazing nation' to regard the Empire as won.[79] It suggested that if England hoped to perpetuate her despotic presence in India, harder work and more self-sacrifice were needed. There was no room for complacency or self-congratulation.

'The Rupaiyat of Omar Kalvin' warned even more directly that English policy in India was bankrupt. Sir Auckland Colvin had been forced to reduce the salaries of government officials in order to balance the budget.[80] The comic portrayal of 'Kalvin' bemoaning the fix he was in revealed that the 'Retrenchment' that he had discovered necessary was symbolic of a much wider malaise:

> Imports are gone with all their Dues –
> Lo! Salt a lever that I dare not use,
> Nor may I ask the Tillers in Bengal
>
> The items of receipt grow surely small;
> The Items of Expense mount one by one.

The last lines of the poem provided a prophecy of England's future cast in lurid, apocalyptic terms:

> [She] Hath cast off Prudence, and her End shall be
> Destruction . . . [81]

These lines, with their references to disappearing imports, destitute farmers and the imminent need to use the hated Salt Tax, focused attention on the real problems of balancing a budget that not only had to serve the domestic administration of the Raj, but had also to finance the larger imperial aims that the metropolitan demanded but would not finance. The state of affairs acknowledged in the poem finds its correlation today in the description by a modern historian of England's Empire in India:

> In essence the Raj depended upon wringing a surplus from an overwhelmingly agricultural economy, and once the costs of empire were met there was very little left for India's development, or to provide for the contingencies of famine and depression.[82]

Like 'The Masque of Plenty', here was a poem that pointed towards crisis: anxiety and anger were implied by the satire. The warning offered implicated both the periphery and the metropolitan.

Such poems as these, however, received no mention in Hunter's review, which was indicative of the total lack of understanding between empire and home country that had been exposed in 'Pagett MP'. More importantly, it was also indicative of the role played by literary institutions in encouraging, at this time, a belief in the rightness of empire, a conviction of racial superiority and a complacency about the way the Empire was run. The reader was guided towards a vision of India that encouraged English self-esteem to grow in the knowledge of the sacrifices made by its sons abroad for the good of others. A man just returned from there assured readers that these poems dealt substantially with the heroism and righteousness of the race. Indeed, the review encouraged the very complacency that the verses had managed to disturb in India.

What is apparent now, however, when this collection is considered alongside the history of its publication and reception, is that it contained some work that was at odds with the imperial discourses of the dominant political groupings at that time. It was the satire of the verses that made reviewers aware of these divergences from the political 'norms', just as it was the satiric mode which caused them most difficulty in seeking an ideological location for the voice/author of the verses. Hunter put the matter most succinctly when he said:

> Mr Kipling handles each situation with a light touch and a gay malice, which makes it difficult to be quite sure whether he sincerely admires his pretty marionettes, or whether he is not inwardly chafing and raging at the people among whom he is condemned to live.[83]

It certainly was far from easy to reconcile many of the attitudes in the verse or affiliate them with the political thinking of the late 1880s. Nowhere was this ambivalence more apparent than with regard to the 'race-thinking' of the collection. The contempt shown for Indians has already been discussed, but its extent is perhaps best gauged by a statement put into the mouth of Dufferin as he retired from office. The experience of India, the reader is led to believe, has turned this respected Whig statesman into a thoroughgoing Conservative, who sees all other races and creeds as inferior to his own:

> You'll never plumb the Oriental mind,
> And if you did it isn't worth the toil,
> Think of a sleek French priest in Canada,
> Divide by twenty half-breeds, Multiply
> By twice the Sphinx's silence. There's your East![84]

The voice within the poem was evidently more than a little tainted by the mid-century lurch towards racism that caused, as Queen Victoria feared, whites to regard Indians as 'niggers'. Racism is used here to justify the status and provide added assurance to the dominant minority. Such thinking was cultivated as part of a general search for group certainty in a community shaken by the emergence of the Congress and the tribulations of the Ilbert Bill. What was strange about Kipling's collection, however, and no doubt was the source of Hunter's puzzlement, was that the contempt for Indians had not been balanced by an exaltation of the English. In the same poem, Dufferin dismissed Anglo-

Indians as 'earnest, narrow men, / But chiefly earnest'. While, therefore, the verses expressed the necessity for a permanent and predatory Raj ['Get guns – more guns'], they held up its chief symbols – the ICS and the Generals – to derision.[85]

There were other attitudes that were equally difficult to resolve. The despotic and militaristic power of the Empire was glorified and encouraged, but the aristocratic pretensions of the ICS were berated and the urgency for radical reform stressed if a crisis was to be avoided. The comedy and satire of the verses undercut any notion that the Englishman had innate status which need not be earned. Some of the verses praised England, but implied that its inhabitants were complacent and/or ignorant. In responding to the lack of certainty produced by these various attitudes, both reviewers, with great determination, presented the collection as songs of an exile, which secured them in a tradition that guaranteed the praise of the nation. Yet this was clearly a strategy that allowed them to avoid the satiric import of the collection. Poems like 'A General Summary', that Hunter did not ignore, he condemned as bad poetry.

This inclination to write-off as bad art observations that were politically unassimilable was to become another recurrent strategy adopted by reviewers in dealing with *Departmental Ditties & Other Verses*. In April 1890, for example, a reviewer in *The Athenaeum* commented that in *Departmental Ditties & Other Verses*, 'the smartness is a little overdone, and the thinly veiled allusions to individuals are often in questionable taste'.[86] Later, the critic described the verses as being those of 'a satirist whose eye is keen', but the parenthesis that followed was a contradiction in terms. He assured the reader that the touch of this satirist was 'seldom other than kindly'. However, kindness is infrequently an attribute of the satirist. The same sort of contradiction occurred again when this 'kindly . . . satirist' was described as writing in an 'Heinesque mood'; again one might add that the inclination of the critic in a mood to expose old and corrupt orders is rarely of a kindly nature. The coolness of response to these verses by the upper strata of Anglo-India had showed that under an autocratic form of government satire was deemed a dangerous weapon. Apparently, in the metropolitan the mode was equally difficult to assimilate at this time. It required the kind of re-adjustment of focus, or reshaping, that Lang and Hunter gave it, or the determined relegation to the second rank with which this reviewer concluded, when he observed that 'Mr Kipling's verse is clever . . . but it is as a prose writer . . . that he will make his literary reputation.'[87]

In a literary culture that allotted the highest esteem to the Romantic lyric, with its criterion of sincerity and its emphasis upon introspection and the personality of the poet, it was, perhaps, inevitable that satire should appear 'questionable'. Kipling was very much aware that both the taste and understanding of the public at this time were determined by their lyric expectations. He prefaced 'La Nuit Blanche', written in 1887, and published in the third edition, with the following lines:

> A much-discerning Public hold
> The singer generally sings
> Of personal and private[88]

Since 'the personal and private' was of little importance in this volume, and less in the ones that were to follow, it was not surprising that in 1893 *The Fortnightly Review* should condemn it, because 'the deeper note' that one could find in Tennyson was entirely absent from the verse. Indeed, it could not be accepted as poetry, it was rather 'a feast of patter songs, dispensed to the twang of the contemporary banjo in the bibulous atmosphere of the post-prandial smoke concert'. Not only was it not poetry, it seems, it was vulgar, and certainly not respectable. At the most it could afford pleasure to the lower orders, 'the domestic commercial clerk, and the suburban young ladies who have lived and loved'. These literary failings, that were also class failings, were rapidly expanded into more generalized and larger failings. The collection betrayed the 'dreadful and slovenly receptivity which is the curse of the clever journalist'. Never was the reader able to 'listen to chords struck in the minor key', because 'Culture' stands to the author '. . . as it did to the author of *Soldiers Three*, merely as "culchaw" '. Consigned to the vulgar and popular, the literary establishment absolved itself of the need to pay critical attention to Kipling's poetry.[89]

What is apparent, however, in both *Departmental Ditties & Other Verses* and in Kipling's *Early Verse*, is that he made deliberate and persistent use of the Janus aspect of satire, while also being discomforted by the insecure relationship this gave him with his audiences. There is in his poetry a constant interplay between narrative and dramatic discourse, so that while the presence of a storyteller is stressed, his point of view is presented as untrustworthy. In the *Bungalow Ballads*, which were written just before the *Ditties*, the reader was told:

> These are the ballads tender and meek,
> Sung by a bard with his tongue in his cheek.
> Sung by a poet, well a day!
> Who doesn't believe a word of his lay.[90]

The effect of the assurance that this is a joke created the suspicion that it was not. 'A Code of Morals' sought to engender the same atmosphere:

Lest you think this story true
I merely mention I
Evolved it lately. 'Tis a most
Unmitigated misstatement.[91]

These kinds of denials were necessary to a satirist, who, aware of the offence his work might give, denied its truth; but for the satiric point to find its mark the denial had to be suspect. This had certainly been the case in Anglo-India, and in England the puzzlement caused by the form, along with the attempts to neutralize the satire, or reject the verse in terms of poor art, all indicated that the collection had caused significant discomfort there too.

Departmental Ditties & Other Verses suggests that the use of the satiric mode arose from Kipling's inability at this time to relate either to the periphery or the metropolitan. In an inscription of 1884, in a presentation copy of *Echoes*, Kipling had written:

Who is the Public I write for?
   Men 'neath an Indian sky
   Cynical, seedy and dry,
Are these then the people I write for?
   No not I.

How should they know who I write for
   Papers that praise me or scoff? –
   More than six thousand miles off
Lives the dear Public I write for,
   Under an English sky.[92]

Biographical explanations which refer to Kipling's yearning at this time for Flo Garrard, or to his dreams of literary success in London, do not account satisfactorily for the speaker's difficulty in relating either to an audience in India or England. His reference to the Anglo-Indian community could hardly be more deprecating, and its newspapers suffer from the same ignorance of which he was to accuse those in the metropolitan. The fourth edition of *Departmental Ditties & Other Verses* was prepared by Kipling shortly after he arrived in England and was introduced by the 'Prelude', a poem that reveals the same kind of hesitancy towards both the periphery and the metropolitan:

I have eaten of your bread and salt,
I have drunk your water and your wine,
The deaths ye died I have watched beside,
And the lives that ye led were mine.

Was there ought that I did not share
In vigil or toil or ease, –
One joy or woe that I did not know,
Dear hearts across the seas?

I have written the tale of our life
For a sheltered people's mirth,
In jesting guise – but ye are wise,
And ye know what the jest is worth.[93]

In one sense, the lines declare Kipling's loyalty to the periphery as he now addresses the metropolitan, but in making the declaration he reveals himself at a distance from both. Although he insists upon his closeness to the colonial community, it is less as a participant and more as an observer who has 'Watched beside . . . the lives that ye led'. In the context of the metropolitan, the Anglo-Indians are no longer the subjects of their own lives, but the objects of narrative interest and he feels obliged to apologize to the 'Dear hearts across the seas' for the 'jest' against them. However, the imputation of ignorance in the 'sheltered people' does not convince the reader either of the poet's respect or empathy with the audience now sought. Indeed, Kipling was soon satirizing the English and their institutions in the same way as he had those of Anglo-India. In a verse letter to his first reviewer, Andrew Lang, Kipling wrote in October 1889:

Now our sun-ward-gazing nation gets its information slick
From the daily mornin' journal – an' it reads darnation quick
So if that information be inaccurately wild
Some eighty million citizens are apt to be beguiled.[94]

Within weeks of his arrival in England, therefore, he felt as distanced from the English as he had done from the Anglo-Indians. Neither, it seems, understood the reality of empire. What lines like these and those in 'The Masque of Plenty' indicate, is an awareness of the changing context in which empire had to be preserved. The coming of the popular press, with its 'information slick', and the emergence in India of an articulate and politically oriented class, altered the atmosphere of political debates. The 'Great Queen' might address India and declare at her Jubilee that:

God hath granted me years
Hath granted dominion and power:
And I bid you, O Land rejoice.

But there were now 'Ploughmen' who could foresee the English Empire going the way of all others:

God raiseth them up and driveth them forth
As the dust of the ploughshare flies in the breeze[95]

Many poems in this collection point to growing apprehensions and dissolving certainties. Their outlook corresponded with those of men like Milner and Chamberlain who feared that England was being eclipsed economically, navally and in other ways. In terms of contemporary debates among historians about imperialism in this period, the verses in this collection align most closely with those who see late nineteenth-century imperialism in terms of a 'siege' mentality, a *Weltpolitische Angst*. Hence, perhaps, the discomfort observable in their reception in India and England.[96]

TWO

'Missis Victorier's Sons'

Barrack-Room Ballads & Other Verses 1889–92

Barrack-Room Ballads & Other Verses, unlike Kipling's first volume of poetry, has not been dismissed as an anachronistic survival of a bygone age. The ballads are well-represented in the most widely available anthologies of Kipling's verse from Faber & Faber and Penguin, and in 1989 Methuen felt confident enough of sales to publish a *Centenary Edition* of the volume, because, it said, these verses remain one of Kipling's 'best known and most widely quoted works'[1] While, however, Kipling's gallery of soldiers seem now to have found a secure place within English culture, they were, initially, given a far more qualified approval. It was not until towards the end of the first decade in which they were published that reviewers were able to feel assured that, although in *Barrack-Room Ballads & Other Verses*, 'The recklessness, the coarseness, the brutality of Tommy Atkins, the spirit of the beast in man, all appear', nevertheless, the collection also revealed 'not less his courage, his fidelity, his sense of duty, his obscure but deep-seated sentiment'.[2] This assurance was derived essentially from the *Other Verses* in the collection, that, increasingly, mediated the *Barrack-Room Ballads* written at an earlier date and published in the newspaper press.

Kipling had arrived back in England in October 1889 after a 7-year stay in India, and, by that time, he was already known to be part of the reading public. As well as the reviews already discussed, *Plain Tales From the Hills* had been published in London in January 1888 and some of the volumes by Kipling included in A.H. Wheeler & Co.'s *Indian Railway Library* had reached these shores and received notices.[3] Nevertheless, Kipling still had his fortune to make. The risk he had taken, in breaking loose from a secure job and trying to succeed in London, had been made possible by a payment of £200 from Wheeler & Co. In return, he had assigned the copyright of the six books in the 'Railway Library'. The business manager of the *Pioneer* had agreed to pay for a series of letters Kipling wrote while en route to and in England and on these resources he struggled to survive, while he tried his hand at earning a living by his writing.[4]

Often, as he makes clear in *Something of Myself*, money was short, and in these early days in England the overwhelming desire and need to make money was a spur. His literary output was a part of a well-organized business campaign, and he used the language of the commercial traveller to describe it. He arrived with 'a stock-in-trade of books', literary output – even that of another – was spoken of as 'merchandise', and he quickly acquired one of the wisest literary agents of the time. During this year, as he wearied himself with an almost endless flow of poetry and prose, 'One thing only stood fast . . . I was making money – much more than 400 rupees a month – and when my Bank-book told me I had one thousand pounds saved, the Strand was hardly wide enough for my triumph.'[5] Ten years later, critics were still impressed by the pecuniary interest that drove Kipling's literary pursuits. Reflecting on his considerable output over the decade, the *London Quarterly Review* remarked that, 'He has been accused of wishing to amass a great fortune.'[6]

Although, however, the immediate personal impulse behind the *Barrack-Room Ballads*, which he wrote mostly in the first 6 months of 1890, was a calculated effort 'to take advantage of the market' and achieve a reputation, these verses indicate that he was also determined, as we saw in his verse letter to Andrew Lang, to educate and undeceive 'the sunward-gazing nation' about its Empire.[7] His poetic critique of the Anglo-Indian ruling elite was now extended to include a much sharper and urgent indictment of metropolitan colonial discourse than that which he had offered in 'Pagett MP'. *Barrack-Room Ballads & Other Verses* represents two quite different poetic means of trying to achieve this end, with different, even contradictory political implications. Kipling owned the distinction between the two types of verses in this volume when he observed in *Something of Myself* that, by the time he wrote 'The Flag of England' in April 1891, he was 'trying to tell the English something of the world outside England – not directly but by implication'.[8] The time that separated the writing of *The Barrack-Room Ballads* from most of the *Other Verses* also involved differences in poetic method. The earlier group of *Ballads* constituted the direct approach to the metropolitan, while the *Other Verses* sought to work at a less explicit, far more self-conscious literary level. Thus, 'The English Flag' strives towards abstraction and symbol, calling on the 'Winds of the World, [to] declare! What is the Flag of England?', while 'The Sons of the Widow' defines the same object in a far more down-to-earth way: 'the bloomin' old rag over' ead' depends upon:

> . . . the stores an' the guns,
> The men an' the 'orses what makes up the
> forces
> O' Missis Victorier's sons.[9]

The verses collected in this volume, therefore, differ significantly in tone, atmosphere and attitudes – and consequently in the reception they received from critics. The *Barrack-Room Ballads* were, as one critic later observed, 'charged with protest' and they showed the same disregard for middle-class values and prejudices as the *Departmental Ditties* had done for the finer feelings of the upper echelons of Anglo-Indian Society.[10] However, the *Other Verses* in contrast to the *Ballads*, although shaped by the same anxiety to link patriotism and empire, so that the latter would be secured, were less populist in their outreach, and acceded to many of the structures of the dominant colonial discourse.

This distinction between the two groups of poems in the volume is borne out by something that W.E. Henley wrote in 1900, 'Concerning Atkins'. Speaking of his publication of the ballads in the *National Observer* he reflected that:

> I do not think they did the journal any good – these songs of the barrack and the march: fresh, vigorous, vecues, surpassingly suggestive as they were, I do not think they did the journal any good. In fact I know they did it none at all. But they were presently collected – [together with *Cleared*, and *Tomlinson*, and *The Flag of England*, to name no more . . .] – into a book; and that book has been for years perhaps the most popular array of verses in the English tongue.[11]

One group of poems, it seems, although widely read, had not found favour with their original readership. However, when mediated and qualified by *Other Verses*, which could be attached to the 'notion' of 'The English Flag', they became more widely acceptable. This response, which, of course, had its parallel with his reception in Anglo-India, originated partly from his failure to fulfil the critical expectations that already surrounded him when he arrived, but, more crucially, from the offence and alarm his verses created in the middle classes, who were to constitute a large section of his readership and of whom he was largely ignorant.

Hunter, it will be remembered, had ignored the more critical aspects of *Departmental Ditties* and recommended Kipling as a poet whose 'very real people' typified the burdensome nature of Anglo-Indian life, where 'heat, solitude, anxiety, ill-health, the never-ending pain of separation from wife and child' were the outer signs of the enormity of the sacrifice made by the England in sharing its culture with subject races and civilizing them.[12] He had led English readers to expect a writer who would confirm the superiority of their own society, while showing at the same time the heroic sacrifice of which the race was capable in the further flung parts of the Empire. Six months later, in *The Spectator*, the reviewer of *Soldiers Three* had found the same reassurance in Kipling's portrayal of Tommy Atkins in India: 'The author does not gloss over the animal tendencies of the British Private, but he shows how in the grossest natures sparks of nobility may lie hid.' The Empire, it seemed, was safe, while guarded by men like Mulvaney, Learoyd and Co. England might take pride in having produced such 'sound and manly' soldiers. The review ended on an enthusiastic note of anticipation: 'The perusal of these stories cannot fail to inspire the reader with the desire to make further acquaintance with the other writings of this author.'[13] Some of the reviewers had, therefore, encouraged their readers to expect from Kipling an uncritical patriotism that would reassure them of their own prestige and of the loyalty and well-being of the Army.

However, quite apart from his anxiety about English imperial strategy and behaviour it is likely, given his youth and long absence from England, that Kipling knew very little about the pride, prejudices and fears of his reviewers and readers. While in India he had been the 'poet of a set', enjoying popularity with those that lived on the periphery of Simla society.[14] In England he was a part of no such community. Besides his uncle and aunts and the introduction he carried to Mowbray Morris, Editor of *Macmillan's Magazine*, Kipling had few social contacts.[15] Least of all did he have much acquaintance with the middle classes, who, as T.W. Heyck has noted, virtually constituted public opinion, and who, at five shillings a volume, must have been the chief purchasers of his work so far.[16] Indeed, in the first year that he wrote in this country, it was the working classes that Kipling had most time to observe closely.

He had taken rooms in Villiers Street and he found himself living above a sausage factory and opposite Gatti's Music Hall. Close by was Charing Cross Station and Villiers Street, of course, gave on to the Strand and then the Embankment. In his first months in this country, therefore, Kipling was in the midst of one of London's busiest thoroughfares, able to observe various groups of working people going about their business: from the costers of the market areas to the warehousemen and the small clerks. It would seem that before Kipling met Henley, and was introduced to the 'little Savile Club', he spent what leisure time he had from his writing in the music halls.[17]

At the time when he lived in Villiers Street, there were at least 18 halls within walking distance, and we know that he visited Gatti's and 'the old Pavvy and Cri'.[18] Moreover, the information that we have about the admission price that he paid suggests that he mixed with the poorer clientele of these places.[19] His visits to the halls, however, were not of the voyeuristic kind of Ewing Ritchie, the temperance missionary who, with all the confidence of the self-righteous man, concluded that the working class he watched in the halls was 'evidently . . . more ready to pay liberally for the gratification of its senses, than for the promotion of its virtues'.[20] Kipling, on his visits to the halls, associated with the working people he met there. He visited Gatti's 'in the company of an elderly but upright barmaid from a pub near by', and 'Among my guests in chambers was a Lion Comique from Gatti's – an artist with sound views on art.'[21] An essay that he sent back to India for publication in *The Pioneer* claimed that 'The halls give wisdom . . . and the people who listen are respectable folk living under very grey skies', although the speaker was equally well aware that gentlemen who 'hold authority in London . . . preached or ordained that music-halls were vulgar, if not improper'.[22]

In the music halls, the master of ceremonies would, though a crescendo provided by the orchestra and his own gavel, introduce the star turn as 'THE GREAT AND ONLY . . .'. Kipling amended only one word of this patter calling his essay 'My Great and Only'. It told of the success of a writer in producing certain verses that wielded an enormous power over the audience that heard them:

> I thought the gallery would never let go of the long-drawn howl on 'soldier'. They clung to it as ringers to the kicking bell-rope. Then I envied no one – not even Shakespeare. I had my house hooked – gaffed under the gills, netted, speared, shot behind the shoulder – anything you please. That was pure joy![23]

The elements of this song are described as 'a refrain . . . four elementary truths, some humour, and, though I say it who should leave it to the press, pathos deep and genuine'; the other essential ingredient was, of course, 'my Great and Only', who, 'with a jingle of brazen spurs, a forage cap over his left eye "could" chuck it off his chest'.[24] A soldier was both the subject and performer of the song, as well as being the key element in the audience that had to be captivated, because 'the redcoat. He has sympathy and enormous boots'. As the speaker watched the effect of his work on 'demented ballet-girls' and 'the now frenzied orchestra', he was led to ask, 'Who shall tell the springs that move masses?', but, to reflect also, 'And the same they say is Vulgarity!'.[25]

This essay, which Kipling sent back to India, bore witness to the great gulf that then existed between working-class and middle-class culture. It is clear from the work of Gareth Steadman Jones and the historians of the music hall, that these places of entertainment, always, as far as the middle classes were concerned, remained beyond the pale. There were efforts to present music hall as an attractive investment, there were efforts to make it respectable by discouraging drink and using the seating arrangements of the conventional theatre – in this way, it was argued, a wider social mix might be encouraged into the halls, but these measures all failed. Music hall remained a working-class institution, and although it was of a defensive and conservative kind, ironically enough it continued to be perceived by the middle classes as a threat to civil order and morality.[26] Ewing Ritchie was typical in judging the music halls 'as idiotic as they are indecent'. He added that:

> The great curse of the age is extravagant and luxurious living, always accompanied with a low tone of public intelligence and morality and thought. In the present state of society we see that realised in the men and women who crowd our music-halls, and revel in the songs the most improper, and in the dances the most indelicate.[27]

The reviews that appeared when the poems were collected into a book echo these attitudes. They indicate that the critics were most offended because 'the author of *Barrack-Room Ballads* takes the music-hall ballads as a model'. One critic noted that the 'cheap effects' of the verse 'were glaring enough to win . . . the applause of the intellectual groundlings, the noisy imperious "pit" of our contemporary theatre of art'. Consequently, another reviewer remarked that the 'Biblical plainness of speech' contained in the *Ballads* was 'impossible to be promulgated at tea-parties' just 'as indeed Thomas Atkins in person would not be an eligible guest at such an assemblage'.[28] The 'vulgarity' of the poems clearly infringed the barrier of respectability which was one of the effective lines of demarcation between the working and the middle classes.

The poems that became known as *Barrack-Room Ballads*, therefore, indicate that the desire to make a statement about Tommy's case and the significance of it in relation to the preservation and continuation of the Empire, was made without any deference to the distance there was between class cultures and the effect it exerted on cultural productions. This distance would, for example, determine the extent and the ways in which the writer for the middle-class audience sympathized with the 'lower orders' and over what. It set limits on the kind of awareness with which other social groups might be credited, and on what knowledge a writer might have about their lives and their indigenous forms and expressions. The attempt in the *Barrack-Room Ballads* to gain acceptance in the drawing-room for what Kipling believed to be the 'sound views of art' that he found in the music hall was bound, therefore, to cause shock and offence. The poems revealed a knowledge about and a sympathy for the soldiers who frequented the halls and an effort to capture 'basic and basaltic truths' in 'observed and compelling songs'. Most disturbing of all, however, they included an attempt to play upon the same emotions, what the reviewer had called the 'cheap effects', that elicited the 'yells, shrieks and wildest applause' of the 'intellectual groundlings', who, in the view of the middle classes, constituted music-hall audiences.[29] Kipling, as P.J. Keating has acutely observed, 'was the first important Victorian writer who was not scared of the working-class'.[30] What must be added, however, if his critical reception and development as a writer are to be correctly understood, is that this courage was not acclaimed. The shocking impact of the ballads was only ameliorated as gradually he became associated with some aspects of the ideology of Englishness. Not until the mid-1890s is the 'doggerel', 'the simple and even vulgar metres and dazzling crudities of speech' of *The Barrack-Room Ballads* allowed to take second place to the 'genius in every line of "The Ballad of East & West" – in almost every line of "The English Flag", and throughout in the stirring "Envoi", a poem that takes you by the heart and shakes you'.[31] Clearly, these verses from the *Other Verses* had played a key role in mediating the shocking impact of the earlier *Ballads* and stirring national sentiment.

The first of the *Barrack-Room Ballads* was published on 22 February 1890, and by June of that year the series was virtually complete. Kipling had already shown in *Soldiers Three* that, in India, 'single men in barricks don't grow into plaster saints'.[32] He was writing about the Army at a time when it had been brought into prominence in the news by the burst of imperial activity in the last quarter of the century. In 1890, the Scramble for Africa was reaching its peak; in the previous decade, 10 million square miles and 100 million people had fallen under European suzerainty. By the late 1880s, maps of Africa in school atlases were revised every year. The attentions of the growing number of war correspondents employed by the press, and the graphic illustrations of its doings published by journals like *The Illustrated London News*, ensured that the Army, which played a key role in Britain's African pursuits, was well before the public eye. Just a year before Kipling began his ballads, this journal ran a series on 'Tommy Atkins – The Private soldier of the British Army – . . . a public servant'. The first item used cartoons and a text to show him well-cared for when sick and, when convalescent, experiencing from 'The little children of married soldiers . . . the endearments of family life'. Later in the series he was shown indulging in horse-play with his fellows, taking part in amateur theatricals, while other drawings showed him well-integrated within the civilian community. During the months in which the ballads were actually published, there was hardly an issue which did not cover some aspect of military life at home and abroad. A battalion was shown buying ponies at Mandalay, officers were seen practising with revolvers and checking stores, new rifles and ammunition were discussed and the military hospital at Chelsea was featured.[33]

However, despite these revelations about heroic exploits, about the respectable domestic behaviour and pursuits of soldiers, and the comforts that surrounded their life in barracks, the Army at home remained unpopular with both the working and the middle classes. Neither felt the affection for the Army that the Press was trying to encourage. The middle classes resented the Army in terms of cost, and because of the age-old threat it seemed to pose should its control fall into the wrong hands. Moreover, the presence of the Army often seemed an offence to respectability, recruiting sergeants haunted public houses, billeting continued into Victoria's reign, and workhouses had more than their fair share of unemployed veterans.[34] Some of the *Barrack-Room Ballads* seemed to be intent on reminding the middle classes of the disruptiveness of the Army within civilian society. The speaker of 'Cells', who 'left my cap in a public-house, my boots in the public road . . . [and] my mark on the Corp'ral's face', and who was arrested 'Mad drunk and resisting the guard' with a head like a concertina, a tongue like a button-stick and a mouth like an old potato, typified all that the middle classes found most offensive and disturbing in soldierly behaviour.[35] Any association with the Army meant immediate and irrevocable exclusion from the middle class. The 'Gentleman-Rankers' have indeed 'lost their way', unable even to write home, they are 'dropping down the ladder rung by rung', cut off from 'all we know most distant and most dear'. As the reviewer had noted, there was no admission for them into the drawing-room.[36]

Neither, however, were the working classes attracted by the Army; they only joined when unemployment was so bad as to offer them no alternative and by the time that Kipling wrote *Barrack-Room Ballads* there was indeed a serious recruiting crisis. During the whole of Victoria's reign, no attempt was made to bring the soldier's pay into line with civilian improvements, and it remained lower than that of the town labourer. The Army taught its serving men no trades, so that at the end of their period with the service they returned to unemployment. General Booth alleged that two-fifths of 2000 destitute men in the East End were former soldiers.[37] The contradiction between the active imperial role of the Army and its poor standing at home in England was inscribed in the chorus of 'Shillin' a Day' – that part of the ballad whose function was to rouse the audience:

> Give 'im a letter –
> Can't do no better,
> Late Troop-Sergeant-Major an' – runs
>   with a letter!
> Think what 'e's been,
> Think what 'e's seen.
> Think of his pension an' –
> GAWD SAVE THE QUEEN.[38]

In 1898, a critic writing about 'Kipling the Poet' made a comment that suggested that *The Barrack-Room Ballads* had not only offended middle-class respectability, but had also awakened its conscience. The reviewer was pleased to note that now, when:

> . . . we think of those multiplying hundreds of God-fearing, clean-living servants of the Queen who have been reached and uplifted through the agency of our own Homes for the Army . . . we cannot resist the strong persuasion that should he write another book on the themes of *Soldiers Three*, Mr Kipling must a little modify the grim colouring of his pictures to suit the changed conditions of the day.[39]

However, when the *Barrack-Rooms Ballads* were first published, they dramatized humanitarian and imperial issues, implying the urgent remedy they required and admitted no concessions to the prejudices of middle-class readers. Rather, through the medium of the heroic recitation ballad, these verses warned that, if the disparity continued between the contempt in which the Army at home was held and the service and sacrifice demanded of it abroad, both the Empire and law and order in England would be in danger. The use of this form was another feature, which, at this time, was particularly associated with the music hall. Kipling's reversal of its characteristic attitudes can only have heightened the threat there appeared to be in the message. Moreover, the message was spoken by rankers, not serving in India but stationed in England, therefore representing a metropolitan view that was approximate to the drawing-room reader, and seemed even to be addressed to him specifically.

Although the heroic recitation ballad was an offspring of the Romantic ballad revival, the enormous expansion and splitting of the reading public in the nineteenth century had facilitated its descent from the literary level to meet and merge with the theatrical and broadside traditions.[40] In their transposition, however, these ballads had not lost their outstanding feature – their nationalistic flavour. A ballad like 'The Lay of the Last Minstrel' was directly concerned to express the strength and loyalty of the nation. In the heroic recitation ballads, current in the music hall when Kipling wrote, this nationalistic flavour was still present as can be seen quite clearly in this version of Charles Godfrey's 'Here upon Guard am I':

> Here upon guard am I,
> Willing to do or die!
> Something is creeping along the way,
> Treachery there is nigh!
> Steady my aim shall be!
> Nearer it crawls to me.
> My trigger I pull it,
> He accepted my bullet,
> He'll never more speak again!
>
> With dauntless heart to war he goes,
> With kindling eyes he meets his foes.
> His flashing sword does ne'er repose,
> When bitter warfare wages.
> He stands in manhood's prime,
> Protecting England's cause sublime,
> His is the bravest and manliest time,
> In Shakespeare's seven ages.[41]

The soldier here is reassuringly affirmed as good and loyal, corresponding to the 'Tommy Atkins' the reviewer had discovered in *Soldiers Three* and the figure depicted in *The London Illustrated News*. The lines try to call forth atavistic responses – the need to defend one's own and the country's honour. They appeal to pride of race, and the undauntable courage of the Englishman, which was always superior to that of foreigners. When Kipling's 'Tommy' is set alongside this, it is not difficult to understand how it would have appeared vulgar and disturbing to middle-class readers, with its inversion of the kind of image of the idealized common man presented by Godfrey, and its use of the techniques and presentation of the recitation ballad popular in the music hall. 'Tommy', the second of the ballads to be published on 1 March 1890, was clearly a response to a question asked in the House by Lord Randolph Churchill on 27 February, and reported in the press. Churchill drew the attention of the Secretary of State for War to an incident that had occurred at Her Majesty's Theatre on 7 January. Three non-commissioned officers of the Royal Horse Guards had been refused entry because they were in uniform. Lord Stanhope had replied that:

> It is intolerable that any disability should attach to wearing the Queen's uniform. I have no direct power in the matter, and the best means of dealing with it effectively requires consideration. But after consultation with the Lord Chamberlain I propose as a first step to send him a memorandum setting forth the views we entertain and he had undertaken to circulate it to theatre's within his jurisdiction.[42]

There the matter ended in the House. 'Tommy' provided the reflection of a soldier, on both the incident and its outcome. The figure who steps forward to speak is not the idealized common man, with stereotypical responses, presented by the the music-hall performers. 'Tommy' speaks in Cockney dialect and transforms the raw news into an 'observed and compelling song':

> I went into a theatre as sober as could be,
> They gave a drunk civilian room, but 'adn't none for me;
> They sent me to the gallery or round the music-'alls,
> But when it comes to fightin', Lord! they'll shove me in the stalls!
> For it's Tommy this, an' Tommy that, an Tommy,
> wait outside;
> But it's 'Special train for Atkins' when the trooper's
> on the tide,
> The troopship's on the tide, my boys, the troopship's
> on the tide,
> O it's 'Special train for Atkins' when the trooper's
> on the tide.[43]

The soldier who speaks here has been able to draw from this occasion certain 'basic and basaltic' truths, not only about the low regard in which he was held by his society, but also about the *real* value he had in it – guarding those who made 'mock o' uniforms', protecting their furthest possessions and being the first to fall 'when there's trouble in the wind'. The basis of Britain's international power and standing, the reason why ''alf o' Creation. . . . Walk wide o' the Widow at Windsor' is that:

> We 'ave bought her the same with the sword an' the flame,
> An' we've salted it down with our bones.
> [Poor beggars! – it's blue with our bones!][44]

Although, at one point the speaker of 'Tommy' stresses his willingness to be patient, if redress is sure, 'We'll wait for extry rations if you treat us rational', by the end of the ballad there is in his voice a clear note of warning, as he tells his reader that 'Tommy ain't a bloomin' fool – you bet that Tommy sees!'[45] These ballads were published a year after the dock strike had warned of the reality of an articulate mass consciousness that might transform the climate of politics.

The note of threat on which the ballad ended, therefore, was magnified by its being cast in a music-hall format. The elements of this ballad, as do those of most of the others in the series, correspond almost exactly with the description of the song in 'My Great and Only', which 'gaffed' the house 'under the gills' so that 'the gallery would never let go' of it. 'Tommy' was built around a refrain, attached to which were 'elementary truths, some humour and . . . pathos . . . deep and genuine'. All the formal attributes that were said to send music-hall audiences into a frenzy, and which the middle classes deemed to be 'Vulgarity', such attributes had been separated out from the traditional sentiments of a song like 'Here Upon Guard am I', and reconnected with feelings of disaffection. This ballad offered a disturbing insight into the potential there was in the *forms* of working-class culture to encapsulate and, in 'netting' the house, to mobilize elements of working-class dissent. Kipling, as we saw, made the same use of the chorus in 'Shillin' a Day', and in 'Loot' the repeated assertion that 'That's the thing to make the boys git up an' shoot!' must have led many to reflect upon the danger that could arise from a disaffected soldiery.[46] In the 1890s, any potential to rouse the masses was a fearful prospect, as the middle classes became increasingly aware of working-class poverty in general, and in particular of the violence and degradation of the lives of the submerged tenth. No wonder that the publication of these verses did the *National Observer* little good.

However, the first of the *Barrack-Room Ballads* that appeared was 'Danny Deever' and its critique was of the Army itself. Like 'Tommy', it employed the eight-line stanza of the traditional ballad, but in 'Danny Deever' the narrative develops from the question and answer form of the type well-known in 'John Randall, My Son'. In itself, this form predicated certain ways in which the subject of the poem could be dealt. The terse questions of 'Files-on-Parade' ('What are the bugles blowin' for?') and the equally abbreviated responses of the 'Colour-Sergeant' ('To turn you out, to turn you out') mean that circumstances and action are given in the baldest terms. However, the effect of this is not one of simplicity or naivety, as might be expected, but of suppressed fear and horror, which, cumulatively, indicates near hysteria in the speakers. It is symbolized in the increasingly irrational answers that the 'Colour-Sergeant' makes to 'Files' . . .' insistent questioning:

> 'What makes the rear rank breathe so 'ard?' said Files-on-Parade.
> 'It's bitter cold, it's bitter cold', the Colour-Sergeant said.

'What makes that front-rank man fall down?', says Files-on-
Parade.
'A touch o' the sun, a touch o' the sun,' the Colour-Sergeant
said.[47]

In this world, where the elements are awry and the natural order inverted, neither cause nor motivation are clear. Danny Deever's condition and crime are only ever presented in generalized terms, which may or may not be true – he is hung 'for a sneakin', shootin' hound' who 'shot a comrade sleepin' '. The reader knows nothing of his reasons for committing the crime, and this increases the nightmare aspect of the whole situation for him, just as Deever's typicality as a soldier implicates all the other soldiers who witness his death. He is one of them, they have slept close to him in barracks and shared his beer, and there, but for the grace of God, go they. This accounts for some of the shocked terror that the men clearly feel at Danny Deever's degradation and hanging. However, the sign of his passing, which recalls that of Christ's, 'black agin the sun', adds another dimension. It is represented as such by 'Files', suggesting that he sees both himself and Deever also as victims, and this symbolic import sits oddly with the military ritual that peremptorily dismisses both the living and the dead:

For they're done with Danny Deever, you can 'ear the quickstep
play,
The regiment's in column, an' they're marchin' us away.[48]

The tripping anapaests here suggest a march and contrast with the grave iambics of the previous stanza. It is a masterly expression of irony – of the body forced to march briskly to a military quick-step while the heart is heavy. Dissonances like this within the poem destroy any sense the onlookers – or a reader – might have had of the justice of the occasion. The deliberate refusal in the ballad of individuality for the protaganists, whether in terms of character, cause or motivation, focuses attention on the brutal ritual of this death and the system that requires a man to die like 'a whipped dog', observed by those who have been his closest companions.[49] The much-repeated refrain, with its heavy stress upon the fact that it is 'they' who are 'hangin' Danny Deever in the mornin', ensures that the reader bears this institutional context constantly in mind.

Into the respectability of the drawing-room, therefore, Kipling had introduced Cockney figures, who bore a startling resemblance to the less reputable elements of a music-hall audience, and who refused to make any concessions either to the company or the surroundings they found themselves in. In these two ballads, the speakers are revealed as being aware of, and alienated from, the brutality of the Army and the contempt in which they were held by the society that Army required them to serve. Two more of these ballads, inspired by their immediate context, add further dimensions to the critique already offered about the relations between military and civilians, home and empire.

'Fuzzy-Wuzzy' appeared a week after 'Tommy', and at a time when opinion in Britain was still very much worried by the possible fate of the British garrison at Suakin. When Britain and Egypt had evacuated the Sudan as the Mahdist power spread, they had managed to retain this Red Sea port, situated at the end of an important caravan route that linked the Sudan with Arabia, India and the East Indies. The Mahdists had been unable to take Suakin, but, whenever circumstances allowed, they charged it, and the garrison was unable to take the offensive until 1891. Again, *The Illustrated London News* had given a good deal of attention to the situation at Suakin. The most lurid engravings showed fierce natives hacked and trampled under foot as they were beaten back by the English cavalry. In the largest prints, it was the officers who were seen winning the day. In smaller insets, however, there were also glimpses of the men with their officers in camp, smoking pipes around campfires as the cook-pots merrily bubbled. Anyone looking at the courage of their fellow Englishmen must have felt a glow of pride and confidence that in the Empire men of all classes were united in its defence.[50]

In contrast, the veteran of the Sudan who speaks in 'Fuzzy-Wuzzy' shows no inclination to praise the qualities of his own imperial race and no pride in the victory that has ensured the continuance of British power. His praise and admiration is for the enemy because:

> We never got a ha'porth's change of 'im:
> 'E squatted in the scrub an 'ocked our 'orses,
> 'E cut our sentries up at Sua*kim*,
> 'An' 'e played the cat an' banjo with our forces.[51]

In 'The Ballad of East and West', the courage of both sides in battle is used to suggest cultural transcendence and the essential brotherhood of all mankind, that:

> . . . there is neither East nor West, Border, nor Breed,
> nor Birth,
> When two strong men stand face to face, tho' they come
> from the ends of the earth.[52]

By way of contrast, in 'Fuzzy-Wuzzy' the essential difference between the two worlds in conflict becomes the basis for an indictment of the victorious English. This difference is shown to be of a technological nature, against which honour and courage are by the speaker recognized to be powerless. The soldier in this ballad is less than proud of a triumph that depended upon superior fire power, for 'We sloshed you with Martinis, an' it wasn't 'ardly fair'; for him, it accentuated the remarkable courage of his 'enemy', who, despite these overwhelming odds, 'crumpled up the square' of British infantry.[53] The emphasis upon technology as the basis of imperial power was repeatedly asserted in *Barrack-Room Ballads* and Kipling was to renew it in his later poetry. At a time, however, when the maintenance and defence of British power was a key national issue, it could not have been comforting to find soldiers whose sympathies lay with their enemies because they believed that they had beaten them by unfair means. After all, speaking here was a representative of 'Missis Victorier's Sons', who was expected to:

> . . . stand by the sea an' the land
> Wherever the bugles are blown.[54]

Yet, he revealed himself as more in sympathy with those he was fighting against, rather than what or who he was fighting to defend. This indication that the British Tommy was not uncritical of his own people and society was confirmed by another of the ballads Kipling wrote at this time.

'Mandalay' was published on 22 June 1890 and is a reflection of a short-term, 'ten-year soldier', about his life in the East compared with his life now in London:

> . . . on these gritty pavin'-stones,
> An' the blasted Henglish drizzle[55]

The images of Burma that the British received from journals like *The Illustrated London News* systematically presented it as an exotic place in the grips of an anachronistic, corrupt regime. There were pictures of the Pagoda at Moulmein, built by the King's bodyguard, of a monster elephant, of Burmese woodcarvers and of the Commander-in-Chief of the Burmese Army in Court Dress. In one issue, accompanying such pictures there was an account of how Britain had removed from power the effete King Theebaw and his wily Queen, replacing their misrule with sound administration. Kipling's ballad, 'Manadalay', with its references to these contemporary images, systematically inverted this dominant discourse of Orientalism, whereby the West was always deemed to be superior to the East. This inversion is heard very clearly in the ex-soldier's assertion that for him every other place and culture is secondary to his experience of the East:

> If you've 'eard the East a-callin', you won't never
> 'eed naught else.
> No! you won't 'eed nothin' else.[56]

Moreover, the rejection of England is made on grounds which seem deliberately chosen to offend English pride, both of place and race. He turns from ' 'ousemaids outer Chelsea . . . Beefy face an' grubby' to his 'Burma girl' who is 'a neater, sweeter maiden in a cleaner, greener land'.[57] Moreover, he presents as preferable those aspects of the Orient that in the West were taken to be evidence of its degeneracy. In Mandalay, the British soldier is free of both the sexual and the moral restraints that Victorian society prided itself on and wished to export to its Empire. The soldier glories in the fact that there, 'there aren't no ten Commandments an' a man can raise a thirst' and kiss a girl 'where she stood'.[58] Once more, in the jaunty, catchy rhythms of the music hall, with refrains that could so easily 'hook' a house, a speaker expressed his disaffection from English society by realigning himself with the subject races of foreign parts. The enthusiasm the working classes were supposed to feel for empire was not evident in these ballads, but worse than that was the indication that they were aware of their oppression and dissatisfied with it.

Therefore, despite the attempts by some reviewers, prior to his arrival, to present Kipling's verse as an uncritical hymn of praise for England, her imperial servants and strategies, he had again shown a disregard for the beliefs of dominant groups and, in the *Ballads*, had written in such a way that any 'reader had to own that good taste is not Mr Kipling's line'.[59] The writer had certainly not fulfilled expectations. Far from providing the reassurance readers had been led to expect, he had, by showing discontented elements within it, raised spectres of political instability in England and native power in the Empire. In this sense, in *Barrack-Room Ballads* he had developed the discourse that had started to emerge in those poems in *Departmental Ditties & Other Verses* which registered anxiety about the security of the Empire and the capacity of its administrators. There, too, he had shown the same disregard for those who might be offended by the burden of the poems. Where the volumes differed was in the more explicit political standpoint incorporated in the poetic form they employed. Satire, although unfashionable in the 1880s, lay firmly within the major literary tradition and indicated a recognition – even if a qualified one – of dominant structures. However, the employment of the ballad, modelled on the current 'patter songs' of the music hall, implied a populism that most of the middle and upper classes found threatening, especially at a time when the electorate was expanding.[60] The basic premise of populism, that virtue resides in simple people and their collective traditions, was epitomized in figures like 'Tommy' with their popular rhetoric. Although this populism had been produced by the author's increasing fear that England might lose her Empire and her position in the world, it could not, in 1889, have appeared other than opposed to the Establishment.

It is with this perspective in mind – of the *Barrack-Room Ballads* suspected by their first readers of being radical, populist expressions – that we should turn to their reappearance in 1892 with the *Other Verses*. The mediated interpellation of the reader that emerges from this volume is initially achieved by the lines dedicated to Wolcott Balestier, that precede all else in the book, even the contents page.[61] They speak of the inheritors of grace, those who have been granted eternal life: 'Beyond the path of the outmost sun. . . . Live such as fought and sailed and ruled and loved and made our world . . .'. Kipling's friend, Balestier, in death it seems is among the Empire builders. There is a clear similarity here between these 'Strong Men' who 'know of toil and the end of toil', and Sir William Hunter's Anglo-Indians serving the Empire in 'heat, solitude and anxiety'. The elect of these verses are in the mould of the public-school Christian 'gentleman unafraid' who from his birth, / In simpleness and gentleness and honour and clean mirth' had done 'his work and held his peace and had no fear to die'. Noticeably, it is only 'gentlemen' who have entered into this eternal dimension; 'Maidens' appear fleetingly and decoratively gracing the table of 'the Gods of the Elder Days'.[62]

In 1892, before a reader encountered anything else, an image was projected of a world under the imminent protection of a secularized 'wise Lord God, master of every trade', who was accompanied by the obedient, those whose 'will [is] to serve or be still as fitteth our Father's praise'. The ballads have been inserted into a pseudo-Christian framework in which eternal life was reserved for 'gentlemen' driven by a high sense of duty, sacrifice and obedience, who never doubted, as 'Tommy' did, that they had served a worthy purpose. These demi-'Gods', who 'knew the hearts of men', were – even in another life – quite literally worlds apart from 'Missis Victorier's Sons'. The 'sentries' of the Empire 'go to a place. . . . Where it's always double drill and no canteen', and may only look forward to 'a swig in hell from Gunga Din'.[63] However, the 'gentlemen unafraid' are in God's confidence, as He 'tells them tales of His daily toil, of Edens newly made', and they speak with him in the language of high literature, not dialect. Spiritual and moral distinctions, it seems, run concurrently with class and gender discriminations.

The major effect of these verses in the 1892 edition was to reveal the existence of a group of natural leaders superior both to those they led and those they conquered. Tommy Atkin's role in the making and keeping of the Empire faded into insignificance. Although Kipling included a dedication, in which he spoke directly 'To T.A.', with the ballads now safely enshrined in a book which only the middle class could afford to buy, and which could be read safely in drawing-rooms, there was little chance of the original ballads appearing in a situation where their dissident potential might be mobilized.[64] Furthermore, the new dedication that Kipling attached to the ballads reduced the urgency of Tommy's case, and its redress was located in an unspecified future in which:

> . . . there'll surely come a day
> When they'll give you all your pay.[65]

The startling impression that the ballads had made on their first appearance, therefore, was now circumscribed at the outset by verses written in a traditional, high diction that bore many features of the dominant Orientalist discourse, that was specifically male-oriented and justified from within a Christian framework cut across by class and racial discriminations. A quite different perspective was cast on verse, which, like that he had written in India, had been deemed to have a subversive potential.

The containment of the ballads was completed by their being equalled in number by as many *Other Verses*. A reader is immediately aware of the formal differences between these earlier and later ballads. Gone is the individuality and idiosyncrasy of the speakers of 'Gunga-Din' or 'Screw-Guns', and they are replaced by the more typical unspecified narrative voice of the traditional ballad, in verses like 'The Last Suttee' or 'The King's Mercy'.[66] The character who emerged from the recitation ballad and spoke of contemporary newsworthy issues that assumed an English setting, was supplanted by the lengthy narrative of incidents, remote in both cultural and historical terms, usually spoken of by anonymous figures, such as 'A Maratta Trooper'.[67] Some of these incidents, like that in 'With Scindia to Delhi', even required prose summaries that preceded the verse.[68] In effect, these formal differences were several. The unlocalized voice of the more traditional ballad with its portentous tones, spoke with an air of generalized importance:

> Boh Da Thone was a warrior bold:
> His sword and his Snider were bossed with gold.[69]

Strangeness and mystery replaced the homely view of the Empire given by the idiosyncratic 'Tommy'. The distancing and objectification of the later poems reduced the soldier's role and, thereby, his claim to reward for it.

However, the most important effect of these *Other Verses* was to re-establish the hierarchies subverted in the *Barrack-Room Ballads*, by providing an alternative emphasis on the power and the superiority of England and the English. The inscriptions of class and rank in the verses to Balestier reassert themselves as the crucial elements in the heroic exploits of empire in the *Other Verses*. The hero of 'The Ballad of East and West' is the Colonel's son; of 'The Three Captains' one was an Admiral, another 'Lord of the Wessex coast and all the lands thereby', and the third 'was Master of the Thames. . . . And Captain of the Fleet'.[70] Significantly, this was the poem in which Arthur Quiller-Couch identified 'genius in every line'.[71] Rankers, however, hardly appear in these later poems; they are described in the most general terms as 'worn, white soldiers in khaki dress', and they certainly do not speak. They are there to endure and die:

> . . . at the Queen's command,
> For the Pride of their Race and the Peace of the Land.[72]

Invisibility and silence ensures their acquiescence in this process, the threats of 'Tommy' and 'The Widow at Windsor' are turned into passive obedience. Soldiers, like their leaders, do their work, hold their peace and have no fear to die, and they certainly experience none of the doubts about the enterprise like the speaker of 'Fuzzy-Wuzzy'. At work here, in 'the Pride of their Race', is a notion of Englishness that incorporates the soldiers through a false sense of homogeneity, thus assuring the reader of their loyalty and readiness to obey orders. The imperial ideology blurred social divisions and underwrote nationalist sentiments. Tommy Atkins as an individualist who is shrewd and can think for himself persuaded English readers that the Army comprised ordinary people like themselves, who, therefore, constituted no threat to civil society. Atkins, rough and ready, but brave and obedient, carrying the latest 'Screw-Guns', convinced them that they were well-guarded by an efficient and modern Army. It is not difficult to see how such a figure might easily be construed as the ancestor of today's professional soldier.

Moreover, where a ballad like 'Mandalay' had suggested a similarity of values between soldiers and the people and society they found in Burma, the English in the *Other Verses* are there to rule and rid these foreign places of semi-barbaric practices like Suttee and ruthless inhabitants who 'filled old ladies with kerosene'.[73] These additional verses, in contrast to 'Gunga-Din' and 'Fuzzy-Wuzzy', suggest that natives are without honour – 'he who held the longer purse might hold the longer life' – so that emphasis then falls on the differences between the English and other races.[74] The 'best' natives are those who recognize their own inferiority compared with the English, and they devote themselves to serving them. This is at its clearest in 'The Ballad of East and West', where Kamal sends his son to the Colonel, telling him:

> Now here is thy master . . . who leads a
> troop of the Guides,

> And thou must ride at his left side as shield on shoulder rides . . .
> Thy life is his – thy fate it is to guard him with thy head.[75]

These 'two strong men' who meet 'face to face' do so as master and servant, not as in 'Fuzzy-Wuzzy' on the equal terms that bring together 'first class fightin' men'.[76] Racial superiority is shown as natural, necessary and awe-inspiring: 'Because on the bones of the English the English Flag is stayed'.[77] By contrasting stereotypes of the English national character and the 'natives' colonial domination is justified.

Finally, of course, this world of imperial enterprise is exclusively male. In 'With Scindia to Delhi', the girl 'bound' behind the hero has, like the other women in these poems, a passive role, she serves to glorify her master's bravery and magnify the sacrifice of his last moments, as 'The darkness closed about his eyes – [and] I bore my King away'.[78] The defining characteristics of the cult of masculinity in these poems are action and individualism: 'We will work for ourself and a woman, for ever and ever, amen.'[79] In 'An Imperial Rescript' and 'Tomlinson', women, books and ideas are all incorporated into the male quest for self-definition through action: 'For the race is run by one and one and never by two and two.'[80] The individualism intimated in these lines not only incorporates women and intellectual activity, it rejects too any tendency towards collectivism, looking to a revival of the old pioneer spirit: 'We're going to hitch our horses and dig for a house of our own.'[81]

The critique of the dominant culture by the *Barrack-Room Ballads* appeared, therefore, by 1892 to have been contained within the more law-abiding framework of the *Other Verses* in which 'the rule of life . . . is that of Law, Duty, Order and Restraint, Obedience, Discipline'.[82] While the *Ballads* were what might be described as an example of the carnivalesque, of the lower orders of society troubling the higher, the addition of *Other Verses* acted as a mediatory link that relocated both in the nation and the Empire. Once this had occurred, the collection became an incident of what Georges Balaridier has called 'The supreme ruse of power . . . to allow itself to be contested *ritually* in order to consolidate itself more effectively.'[83]

Certainly, the racy, colourful speech of Kipling's soldiers challenged the conventional poetic rhetoric of the literary institution. Its bounds were broken by the soldiers' alliterative parallelisms, with the elephants labouring in the 'sludgy, squdgy creek' at 'Mandalay', by their word coinages as 'time-expired' men, and by their slang-forms to refer to 'the Great Gawd Budd' or by their wonderfully luxuriant metaphors in which India was evoked with a heat that made the 'eyebrows crawl'.[84] This style relied only superficially on Cockney dialect and far more on the imaginative use of the popular language of the music hall and the barracks. Such a usage of language inverted official words and hierarchies, so that 'The English Flag' was a 'bloomin' old rag', the day of battle was the 'Widow's picnic', Atkins was killed by the carelessness of his officers and the native was ecstatically revered as ' 'E's a daisy, 'e 's a ducky, 'e 's a lamb'.[85] This vision of the Empire, seen from below, registered the same scepticism and hesitancy that historians have discovered in working-class response to it. Indeed 'Tommy' recognized himself as a primary site of contradiction: as both reviled and desired, as rejected and accepted as necessary. Owned and disowned, he is both other and self, a symbol of the fusion in late Victorian society of power, fear and desire.

However, although in these *Ballads*, as in most examples of carnival, 'The cheerful vulgarity of the powerless is used as a weapon against the pretence and hypocrisy of the powerful', the reviewers ensured that it was only to the extent that the verses became 'a statement of Tommy's case as powerful and convincing as it is passionate and sincere'.[86] The implications of the poems, as they were commented on in the journals, were not allowed to extend beyond humanitarian and literary considerations; then, by considering the *Other Verses*, it was possible to assure readers that 'The dominant tone of the work is patriotic; and it is the tone of the new patriotism, that of imperial England, which holds as one all parts of her wide-stretched empire, and binds them in the indissoluble bond of common brotherhood.'[87] The spectres raised by the *Ballads* and subdued by *Other Verses* underlines the obvious but often ignored truth that the carnivalesque is not intrinsically radical or conservative. Its political effect cannot be assigned outside its literary and historical conjunction, 'there is no *a priori* revolutionary vector to carnival or transgression'.[88] Furthermore, because the *Barrack-Room Ballads* were descended from a form of carnival, the music-hall, that was essentially 'a licensed affair . . . a permissible rupture of hegemony', the carnival laughter 'of the *Ballads* was ultimately' incorporating as well as liberating'.[89] Other *Verses* merely provided the structures that ensured the reassimilation of a disaffected soldiery and the working class from which it was drawn.

Richard Shannon has remarked in *The Crisis of Imperialism 1865–1915* that 'The characteristic "Englishness" of English culture was . . . invented in the last quarter of the nineteenth century.'[90] A collection of poetry such as *Barrack-Room Ballads & Other Verses* shows how religion, class, race and gender could be re-inscribed so that notions of Englishness were confirmed and nationalist sentiments were underwritten. Throughout this collection there is present the same anxiety, as in *Departmental Ditties & Other Verses*, to strengthen and preserve the

Empire and to alert the metropolitan to the changed conditions in which imperial power had to be maintained. Whereas, however, in the Anglo-Indian verse there was a concentration on governmental incompetence, growing native awareness and economic bankruptcy, the preoccupation of *Barrack-Room Ballads & Other Verses* was with military and technological mastery as the only way of ensuring the continuation of English power. Cumulatively, the preoccupations indicated an increasing conviction that all was not well with imperial and national strategy.

However, this growing anxiety was matched by a dilution in both the kind and the content of the critique of contemporary imperial strategy that Kipling's verse contained. While the *Barrack-Room Ballads* are distinguished from the *Departmental Ditties* by the vitality of their poetic means, it was a vitality whose source was soon abandoned. The ballad model, based on music-hall practices and the colloquialism of popular speech, gave way to the traditional ballad and to a high diction more acceptable in the Victorian drawing-room. This transition to *Other Verses* corresponded with an abandonment too of the populist strain that had begun to emerge in *Departmental Ditties* and developed significantly in *Barrack-Room Ballads*. In both collections, the populism was a symptom of the distance the writer felt from centres of power. In reaction, the verse located true perspicacity in simple people, such as natives and soldiers. An amalgam of personal phobias and political anxieties, this distance had, nevertheless, decreased sufficiently by the time some of the *Other Verses* were written, for those principles rejected in India and interrogated in *Barrack-Room Ballads* to be reconfirmed.[91] This affirmation was seized upon by the reviews so that any rites of reversal in *Barrack-Room Ballads* ultimately preserved and strengthened the late Victorian established order.

THREE

'So long as The Blood endures'

The Seven Seas 1896

Before Kipling's third volume of verse, *The Seven Seas*, was published at the beginning of November 1896, there were 22,000 subscribers. Two months before, Queen Victoria had completed the sixtieth year of her reign and in the ensuing months preparations got under way to celebrate, in the summer of the following year, what became known as the Diamond Jubilee. A decade previously, in 1887, when the Golden Jubilee had commemorated 50 years of Victoria's rule, most of the royalty of Europe had come to London and witnessed a great show to Britain's wealth and military strength. Ten years later and ten years older, the Queen was no longer able to bear the stress that such regal entertainments placed upon her and she readily accepted the suggestion that the Diamond Jubilee should be so framed as to emphasize the extension of the Empire which was now recognized to be one of the most imposing characteristics of her sovereignty. Accordingly, it was arranged that prime ministers of all the colonies, delegates from India and the dependencies, and representatives from all the Armed Forces of the British Empire should take a prominent part in the public ceremonies.

Reviewers of *The Seven Seas* immediately stressed that the collection belonged within this celebratory imperial climacteric. Kipling, said one critic, had 'seized upon the unspoken national thought and enshrined it in imperishable verse'.[1] This collection, declared another, was a work of 'passionate, moral, imperial patriotism', that would contribute 'in strengthening the foundations of England's influence and . . . fame'.[2] The poems in this volume – which, among other things, laid a heavy emphasis upon 'The Pride of the Race'[3] – could clearly be related to the moment when thousands thronged the 6-mile route in London on 22 June to catch a glimpse of the aged Queen, who had reigned longer than any other English sovereign, and who, as she left the palace, had sent a telegraphic greeting to all parts of the Empire which thanked her 'beloved people'. A year later, one of the journals was still remarking on the way that *The Seven Seas* had captured 'the national spirit'. *Blackwood's Magazine* suggested:

> It is surely no vain imagination to suppose that the Jubilee rejoicings of last year possessed a deeper significance and were informed with a more exalted spirit than those of ten years before. The soul of the nation seemed to be more profoundly stirred. Ideas and aspirations of a loftier order seemed to have taken root in the nation's heart. And if such indeed were the case, it was to Rudyard Kipling more than to any other writer that the change was due, just as it was he who seized upon the unspoken national thought and enshrined it in imperishable verse.[4]

The author who had been, as this critic admitted, previously considered 'flashy' and 'irritating' was now seen to reflect 'a fine sense of national honour'.[5]

In the anthologies of Kipling's poetry available now, both compiled when there was less enthusiasm for empire and less confidence in the vigour of the English race, *Departmental Ditties & Other Verses*, whose subjects were imperial, fared badly, as we saw. The songs of *The Seven Seas*, in contrast, remain very much to the fore: they constitute between 17 and 20 per cent of the total number of poems included. Moreover, many of the poems which were singled out for special attention by their contemporary reviewers are among the ones chosen by the anthologists, suggesting that their ideas and assumptions about being British still in some ways resonate.

Structurally, *The Seven Seas* resembled Kipling's preceding volumes of poetry in that it included two sections. The first gave its name to the book as a whole. However, in the previous collections, the second group of poems was gathered under the title *Other Verses*, but in *The Seven Seas* there was another set of *Barrack-Room Ballads*. This second group of poems was significantly smaller than the first – it contained half the number of poems, and it occupied only 30 per cent of the space in the collection. In terms of appearance, therefore, the vernacular articulations of 'Missis Victorier's Sons' were clearly relegated to second place, which seemed to confirm the readjustment of perspective that, in the earlier volume, *Other Verses* had effected.[6] Reviewers certainly devoted most prose and space to the first group of poems, but some of them found it necessary to question the appropriateness of the inclusion in this volume of further soldier songs which they found 'full of dirty and repulsive detail'.[7] Not everyone, it seems, was entirely convinced by the visible reassurance that conventional poetic rhetoric and social structure had been confirmed by *The Seven Seas* group of verses.

The first poems, however, in no way defied the conventional expectations of a middle-class reader, they approached their audience via a discourse laden with religious overtones. The speaker of the 'Dedication' expressed himself in reverential terms, thanking God for 'Strength above [his] own' and, frequently, both the sentiment and the line common to the hymn were used.[8] 'A Song of the English', which assured readers that England's 'pathway to the ends of all the Earth' was the work of 'the Lord our God Most High' began 'Fair is our lot – O goodly is our heritage!', a line that might easily have found its way into *Hymns Ancient & Modern*.[9] Some reviewers were quick to note 'the devout recognition' in this volume of 'the Hand that rules England' and, on the strength of it, to conclude that, 'Mr Kipling has made great advances as a serious poet since the appearance of *Barrack-Room Ballads*'.[10] Within a year of the publication of *The Seven Seas*, it was accepted by some groups of readers and critics as a celebration of the achievements of the metropolitan spirit, of essential Britishness.

In other obvious ways these poems, which considered how 'We've painted the islands Vermilion', differed in both focus and purpose from the verses in either of the earlier volumes.[11] Fewer individuals stepped forward to speak or be spoken about. The concern was with the larger processes of empire. Emphasis was laid upon the importance of both the mercantile and strategic aspects of imperial activity, which, in their turn, implicated problems of defence:

> . . . the ships of England go!
> Swift shuttles of an Empire's loom.[12]

But their business was shown to be dependent upon holding places such as Singapore:

> East and West must seek my aid
> Ere the spent gear may dare the ports afar.
> The second doorway of the wide world's trade
> Is mine to loose or bar.[13]

Trade and empire were therefore inseparable, because of the latter, 'The Merchantmen' were able 'to bring a cargo up to London Town'. Empire was not incidental to England's worldwide interests but central.[14]

Obviously, lines such as these seemed particularly appropriate during 2 weeks when London celebrated its sense of its own greatness, as the metropolis of a far-flung Empire. However, the intention a writer has in producing their work and the use to which it is put when it becomes publicly available are often quite different. Such a difference would appear to have existed between Kipling's aim in writing the verses included in *The Seven Seas* and the celebratory use to which they had been put. The 'Recessional' hymn, published on 17 July 1897 at the end of the Diamond Jubilee celebrations, attempted to make this gap between the two apparent. It deliberately sought to disengage itself from that particular historical moment and re-establish a connection with the larger discursive formation and the poetry by Kipling that was already a part of it.

Most of the poems in *The Seven Seas* had been written while Kipling was living in Vermont, commuting annually to England, often via circuitous routes that took him to the further reaches of the Empire. On the domestic front, Kipling saw from afar the comforts bestowed by the great consumer boom, but also the continuation of the social restlessness of the 1880s, as culture and politics struggled to adapt itself to mass audiences. There was 'an explosion of working-class consciousness' that expressed itself in the revival and transformation of the trade union movement.[15] By 1893, the Independent Labour Party had been founded and Keir Hardie elected to Parliament: 'Labour had emerged from the status of a social issue to a political issue.'[16] In terms of the traditional parties, it was a period of Conservative ascendancy. Nevertheless, a new Liberal critique was emerging, despite the conversion to imperialism of Rosebery and others prominent in that party. By 1889, Hobson had already formulated his theory of domestic underconsumption that nominated imperialism as a great social evil.[17]

The years between Kipling's settling at Brattleboro in 1892 and his return to England in 1896 were eventful ones for the Empire. There was a considerable amount of English imperial activity on the Niger and in Egypt and, in 1895, Joseph Chamberlain became Colonial Secretary. He was soon involved in the Venezuelan Crisis with the USA, which occurred during Kipling's last year in Vermont, and the better known Jameson Raid. The dispute with the USA had arisen over Venezuela's claim to be part of British Guiana, on the basis of ancient rights derived from Spain. President Cleveland, probably in an attempt to boost his election prospects, issued an ultimatum which appointed an American Commission to determine just boundaries. Suddenly, there was the possibility of war, if England were asked to relinquish territory it thought of as its own and the USA sought to enforce any decision by the Commission.

The press in England talked of Sikhs and Gurkhas for British Guiana, and in America Theodore Roosevelt observed that '. . . in the long run this means a fight. Personally I rather hope the fight will come soon. The clamour of the peace faction has convinced me that this country needs a war.' As Garvin acidly remarked, in his biography of Chamberlain, 'the emotions of what is called imperialism' were by no means confined to England at this time.[18] Kipling was 'sick and sore and sorry to my heart's core' at this prospect of war between those who he still saw as members of the same family.[19] It was at this point in late December 1895, at the height of the Venezuelan Crisis, that Dr Jameson made his attempt 'to filibuster the Transvaal Republic into the British Empire'.[20]

The phenomenal rise of the Boer Republics to an economically dominant position in South Africa had threatened British paramountcy and made the looked-for union of the colonies increasingly unlikely. There was also a security issue at stake – the all-important Cape route to India. In this situation the government gave ear, but not sanction to Rhodes' ideas about an invasion to overthrow the Boer Republic. The plan came to nothing, but Dr Leander Starr Jameson decided to go ahead, leading a column of 600 troopers into the Transvaal. The result was a disaster: the 'campaign' lasted 4 days and ended in ignominious surrender to Kruger's forces.

Chamberlain condemned the affair, but his knowledge about it remains to this day a matter of dispute; however, the firmness and conciliatory expertise with which he resolved the dispute over Venezuela helped to restore his political and public reputation. Convinced, not surprisingly in view of the South African affair, that at this time there was no 'people from whom we can afford to accept a kicking', but alive also to the 'inflammable gases of anti-British feeling', he managed to negotiate a settlement that guaranteed territory occupied by British people for 30 years or more.[21] The handling of this affair by the new Secretary of State for the Colonies certainly impressed Kipling, more so perhaps because of the similarity there was between the ideas he had expressed in his verse in *The Seven Seas* and Chamberlain's desire to strive for the federation of the Empire. Both of the recent disputes had brought home to many the isolation of Britain and the enormous defensive problems it faced if there should be simultaneous unrest in South Africa, or anywhere in the Empire, as well as German ill-will in Europe.

It was via this formation, from within the setting of another culture that had not only recently rejected English control but deliberately challenged it, that the poems in *The Seven Seas* and the 'Recessional' meditated on the subject of empire. The warning in the latter, therefore, that when 'The tumult and the shouting dies . . . all . . . pomp / Is one with Nineveh and Tyre', was a reminder of what imperialist historians of the 1890s recognize as the 'false impression . . . well-known to be false by many of its purveyors' of 'immense national self-confidence'.[22] It recalled 'What the People [of India] Said' in *Departmental Ditties &*

Other Verses about the Jubilee of 1887. The 'Ploughmen' had reflected on the transitoriness of all previous empires implying quite clearly that the English one might be of the same order.[23] Moreover, the 'People' of 'Recessional', 'drunk with the sight of power', capable of 'frantic boast and foolish word', suggested not only the overweening pride of the nation as a whole, but that possibility of a mass consciousness that could transform the entire climate of politics that the articulacy of the soldiers in *Barrack-Room Ballads* had raised.[24]

If, however, the 'Recessional' recalled the anxieties of previous volumes, the purpose behind its reprimand was not merely – as many commentators seemed to think – to teach the lesson of humility, but to intimate that there was, as the verses in *The Seven Seas* had tried to show, a different and more urgent conception of 'Dominion over palm and pine'.[25] The congratulatory atmosphere engendered by the Jubilee, and the association of the collection with it, had obscured the clear attempt in this volume, not merely to confirm, but to remake English imperial identity based upon a unity of 'the men of the Four New Nations / And the Islands of the Sea', bound together in a semi-mystical faith at 'our dread high altar / Where The Abbey makes us We'.[26]

The Seven Seas was a highly charged instance of what Bernard Porter has called the 'new' or 'visionary' imperialism, called into being in the 1890s as Britain faced a more hostile and aggressive world, economic setbacks and increased electorates. The essential characteristic of this outlook was that it 'did not merely accept the empire as a necessary expedient of British foreign policy, but wished to build upon it a whole new order of things, which was to be fundamentally different from what had gone before'.[27] It found several very powerful and persuasive political advocates. In 1885, Lord Milner, in an election speech at Willesdon, offered this vision of the *Pax Britannica* to his audience:

> Let us always remember that in speaking of our country we do not mean merely these islands. We mean every land inhabited by men of English race living under English institutions. . . . I think we can foresee a time when the great Anglo-Saxon Confederation throughout the world, with its members absolutely self-governing in their domestic concerns, but firmly united for purposes of mutual protection, will not only be the most splendid political union that the world has even known, but also the best security for universal peace.[28]

However, the 'new' imperialism found its greatest political advocate in Joseph Chamberlain who, as far back as 1886, had begged in vain from Gladstone the office of Colonial Secretary. When Salisbury offered him the post in 1895, he made it clear to Chamberlain that a higher post was his for the asking, but for the Birmingham MP the Colonial Office provided the opportunity to fulfil his imperial vision that no other post could: 'I said again I should prefer the Colonies – in the hope of furthering closer union between them and the United Kingdom'.[29] In 1895, he believed 'in the practical possibility of a federation of the British race'. Chamberlain argued that if this 'Greater Britain remains united, no empire in the world can ever surpass it, in population, in wealth, or in the diversity of its resources'; with the achievement of such a federation Britain might 'have confidence in the future'.[30] Such a unity was dependent not only upon political and economic arrangements, but also on the present generation realizing that it must be:

> . . . our task, to keep alight the torch of Imperial patriotism, to hold fast the affection and confidence of our kinsmen across the seas, that so in every vicissitude of fortune the British Empire may present an unbroken front to all her foes, and may carry on even to distant ages the glorious traditions of the British flag.[31]

During his first 2 years as Secretary of State for the Colonies, between July 1895 and the Colonial Conference held during the Jubilee celebrations of 1897, Chamberlain lost no opportunity to expand upon this federationism, which, paradoxically, like the 'Recessional', also had its undercurrent of uncertainty and apprehension. At another time, Chamberlain had reflected in a speech at a banquet in the Imperial Institute, that:

> We are all prepared to admire the great Englishmen of the past . . . but when it comes to our own time we doubt, we seem to lose the confidence which I think becomes a great nation such as ours.[32]

Where Chamberlain used political rhetoric to try to foster the 'Imperial patriotism' that would open the way to federation and, hopefully, combat self-doubts and the diplomatic and commercial crises, the poetry of *The Seven Seas* attempted the same task by exploiting collectively shared symbols: symbols that called upon uncritical emotional responses in order to re-invent English identity and history. Whereas *Departmental Ditties* had attempted this end via a satiric critique, *The Seven Seas* reversed the process and praised the achievement so far in order to inspire a future one. Both collections were, however, inspired by an ideal that was yet to be achieved and were preoccupied by the changing world context of empire at the end of the nineteenth century.

The new version of English imperial identity, although permeating the volume as a whole, was particularly evident in the sequence called

'A Song of the English', which, significantly, opened the collection. The poem begins with the quite deliberate use of the language of the Bible and the metre of the hymn to characterize, as a departure from 'righteousness', the lukewarm attitudes of Liberals towards the Empire. These 'evil counsellors' with whom 'the Lord shall deal', have caused the country to stumble and stray from its real 'heritage . . . a pathway to the ends of all the Earth!' Clearly, therefore, for England to fulfil the destiny expressly designed for it by 'the Lord our God Most High', it must reject the 'dishonour' of anti-imperial policies, 'Whoring not with visions – overwise and overstale' – the latter, no doubt, a reference to Gladstone's great age and the image his enemies pedalled of him as a dry-as-dust rationalist, overwhelmed by his own learning, who had shown in his home rule policy an incapacity to appreciate the fervour with which people clung to their national identity.[33] As the poem proceeds, imperialism becomes synonymous with the Christian faith and all that is to be revered in English history, so that readers were exhorted to 'Hold ye the Faith – the Faith our Fathers sealed us'. The final imprecation to 'Keep ye the Law' implied the necessity for imperial man to accept leadership and authority, to 'be swift in all obedience', and to understand that sound character and true identity was found in a life of action:

> Clear the land of evil, drive the road and bridge the ford.
>   Make ye sure to each his own
>   That he reap where he hath sown;
> By the peace among our peoples let men know we serve the
>   Lord![34]

Here, it is the engineer not the soldier who blazes the trail to colonization, and it is not difficult to identify the assumptions which govern these lines – that since the indigenous people have achieved none of these ends they are not equals. They are not members of the same moral order as the civilized, but people whom time has left behind and whose ignorance holds in check the expansion of the world's resources that men of energy can exploit. Through the use of religious rhetoric in these verses, imperialism is represented in the way that Lord Milner described it, as having 'all the depth and comprehensiveness of a religious faith'.[35] While this rhetoric undoubtedly represented the strength of Kipling's own commitment to the Empire, it must also, by equating it with Conservatism and Christianity, have made empire a more marketable commodity for some middle-class readers.

Sandwiched between these opening verses and the next sequence, 'The Song of the Dead', was a short poem, 'The Coastwise Lights of England'.[36] It showed the Empire as a vast commercial enterprise produced by an island identity whose first need was to trade. The position of this poem, however, indicated a desire to suborn the aggressive economic thrust of imperialism 'the clippers . . . that race the Southern wool', to the moral mission of the colonialist who emerged in the next song as a fully fledged noble adventurer.[37] We read in 'The Song of the Dead' that:

> We were dreamers, dreaming greatly, in the man-stifled town;
> We yearned beyond the sky-line where the strange roads go down.
> Came the Whisper, came the Vision, came the Power with the Need,
> Till the Soul that is not Man's soul was lent us to lead
> As the deer breaks – as the steer breaks – from the herd where they graze,
> In the faith of little children we went on our ways.
> Then the wood failed – then the food failed – then the last water dried –
> In the faith of little children we lay down and died
> On the sand-drift – on the veldt-side – in the fern-scrub we lay,
> That our sons might follow after by the bones on the way.
> Follow after – follow after! We have watered the root,
> And the bud has come to blossom that ripens for the fruit!
> Follow after – we are waiting by the trails that we lost,
> For the sounds of many footsteps, for the tread of a host.
> Follow after – follow after – for the harvest is sown:
> By the bones about the wayside ye shall come to your own![38]

These lines are preceded by a call to 'Hear now the Song of the Dead', which encourages reverence and respect for the early empire builders by engaging the attention of the reader with vicarious sensational involvement. The references to 'the torn berg edges . . . the sere river courses . . . the heat-rotted jungle hollows' is there to inspire pride in imperial expanse; the exotic is introduced where 'the warrigal whimpers and bays' and the tragic appears in 'the waste that betrayed them'.[39] However, it is in the lines quoted that the effort to create an imperial enthusiasm reaches a new crescendo.

The Englishman who leaves 'the man-stifled town' is transformed and takes on near god-like proportions as he embarks on the colonial enterprise and 'the Soul that is not Man's soul was lent us to lead'.[40] The English, clearly, were chosen to govern, with all the superior attitudes towards native cultures that such an assumption involved. Moreover, the line that describes the coming of the urge to empire, 'Came the Whisper, came the Vision, came the Power with the Need', mimics biblical accounts of the descent of the Holy Spirit, thereby reintroducing the equation already established between Christianity and the Empire and confirming the moral superiority of the English.[41] Further Christian parallels are insinuated within these lines. The early settlers are represented as 'little children', whom Christ had identified as the truly pure and innocent who would inherit the kingdom of God. The refrain

> Follow after – follow after! We have watered the root
> ....
> Follow after – we are waiting, by the trails that we lost.[42]

recalls Whitman's 'O Pioneers', but whereas his use of the refrain is as an apostrophe of awe and admiration, the imperative here is propagandistic, it seeks to encourage an emotion that can only be discharged in action. Its intention is to produce the illusion of immanent ancestral presences who deserve praise and emulation. The English of the past in alien lands take on historical respectability and justification and their descendants can bask in their glory, while readers in the metropolitan can be proud of their kinship with such people. Past and present are in this way brought together as parts of the great future whole of empire and the linkage becomes the recovery and assertion of a consensus between the living and the dead. The final section of this part of the poem, which dwells upon 'blood' as 'the price of admiralty', reiterates the special relationship in imperial history between past and present, kin and kin.[43]

The great drive behind this urge to empire, now, and 'When Drake went down to the Horn / And England was crowned thereby', has been 'Adventure', which made heavy demands on the heroic virtues of its protagonists.[44] The portrayal of the empire builder as a noble adventurer, besides asserting racial superiority and ensuring the subordination of 'native character', also provided a vivid contrast with the Anglo-Saxons described in *Departmental Ditties & Other Verses*, who went to India because it was a place where one earned more and spent less, because jobs were guaranteed, wages high and careers more rapid. Even the resolute civil servants Hunter described, sticking to their posts through heat and solitude, seemed less admirable and certainly less exciting than 'The Gentlemen Rovers abroad' who 'broke the road for the rest'.[45]

The 'Vision' of the Greater Britain in this section of the poem acknowledged two empires – the confederation of the Dominions and Great Britain and the Dependent Empire (the Crown Colonies and Protectorates). In 'The Song of the English', the latter had a small role and the verse had nothing to say about the problems and contradictions involved in trying to bind two such empires 'close in the indissoluble bond of common motherhood'.[46] To lay such a heavy emphasis on the kinship between Britain and the Dominions was to increase the problems of imperial unification. Such racial exclusiveness suggested that, whenever strength and unity were under consideration, reliance could only be placed upon the British element, and this was bound to have given offence to most of the Dependent Empire. Aware, perhaps, that such an impression might arise from the 'Song of the English', the verses called 'The Native Born' showed great anxiety to recognize the loyalty of those who:

> . . . change their skies above them,
> But not their hearts that roam![47]

This poem – as did also 'The Flowers' – reprimanded 'English brothers' for their insularity, for failing to understand that:

> . . . our faith and our hope and our honour
> We pledge to our native soil![48]

When the perspectives of both poems are taken together, it is by no means clear how the federation of the Dominions and Dependent Empire could occur alongside the insistence upon racial exclusiveness – though in the event it was the sensitivity of the Dominions to what they regarded as infringements upon their national independence that prevented any kind of federation at this time.

Actively pursuing the propagandist impulse – to create an imperial enthusiasm – the next phase of this sequence, 'The Song of the Sons', imagined the beginning of the new age. England, the 'Mother', was 'From the whine of a dying man, from the snarl of a wolf-pack freed'.[49] Once more this was a bitter reference to the previous political dominance of the Liberals, now seen to be at an end with the passing of Gladstone, who had retired and was dying from cancer – though still sending forth some astringent political comments. The new political era, in contrast with the old, was to be one of integrity and honour. A government which lent 'our hearts for a fee' would be replaced by one that worked 'without promise or fee' and whose great purpose would be to seek kinship with all those 'that were bred overseas'. If the 'Mother' will only be 'proud of thy seed' and 'Judge' that her sons 'are . . . men of The Blood', then she could be assured that 'the world is thine'.[50] This short movement, like the one at the beginning and that which was to follow, were reminders that 'The Song of the English' combined Swiftian political satire with the attempt to teach the nation to think imperially.

Indeed, the final section of this long poem, called 'England's Answer', contained an emphatic reminder that in 1893, when it was written, this imperial enthusiasm was still to be achieved. At the end, emphasis falls not only on 'Vision' but also on an urgent 'Need'. England was represented by the image of the 'grey mother', who is cast in the role of a supplicant. However strong 'her' own commitment to federation, she obviously realizes that 'she' has to persuade those 'Little used to lie down at the bidding of any man' of its merits, even though they are 'Flesh of the flesh that I bred'. In the end, the only incentives she is able to offer are her own convictions of kinship, the facilities to 'talk together, brother to brother's face' and the prospect of unity at some future biblical rendezvous:

> . . . So long as The Blood endures,
> I shall know that your good is mine: ye shall
>   feel that my strength is yours:
> In the day of Armageddon, at the last great fight.

The rather nebulous exhortations to 'stand to your work and be wise', and this futuristic vision, were curiously prophetic of what did occur in 1897 when just such a colonial conference as the one imagined here took place.[51]

During the fortnight of the Diamond Jubilee celebrations, Chamberlain arranged five meetings attended by the 11 premiers of the independent colonies. The issue to which, of course, he directed their attention was 'that of closer relations . . . Federation . . . for the maintenance and protection of imperial trade all over the world'.[52] At the first meeting, the assurance that Chamberlain was able to give his audience that 'In this country, at all events, I may truly say that the idea of federation is in the air', could have owed something to the verses in *The Seven Seas*, which had concentrated on arousing such enthusiasm for the idea and which by the time of the Jubilee had sold three editions.[53] However, the lack of certainty the Colonial Secretary felt about 'whether with you it has gone as far' suggested that this enthusiasm was one-sided, and his admission that there was 'a real necessity for some better machinery of consultation between the self-governing colonies and the mother-country . . .' echoed the supplications of 'England's Answer'.[54] In 1897, the 'Vision' of the new imperialists was still some way off. Moreover, the negative response of the Conference left the idea of federation in the future as unlikely as ever. Chamberlain noted in his final speech that 'Conference . . . has undoubtedly rejected . . . the proposal for a

Zollverein with free trade in the British Empire'.[55] Neither had it been willing to strengthen imperial defence or to consider political forms of representation for members from the colonies. Sadly, Chamberlain observed to Devonshire that these men were 'Premiers first and patriots second'.[56] All of them had feared that confederation would cost too much, would infringe their independence and development and, ultimately, only benefit England.

The hesitancy at the end of 'The Song of the English' and the failure of the Jubilee Conference are a reminder that, although in the 1890s the 'visionary' imperialists were in positions of authority, although with Kipling's popularity alone, they had access to a great number of people, nevertheless, they failed to achieve their *political* aim of federating the Empire and placing it at the forefront of foreign and commercial concerns. And, while the 'Recessional' had claimed a distinction between 'visionary' imperialism and the 'tumult and shouting' of a crowd enthused by the mere spectacle of empire, it was arguably a tenuous distinction. Ultimately, both types were dependent upon 'The Pride of Race', and the celebration in *The Seven Seas* of imperial achievement – for whatever reason – confirmed and supported a whole range of discourses which, in the late nineteenth century, cut across class lines and asserted the right of England to colonize and govern the world.

In his memoirs, for example, Kennedy Jones, Editor of *The Daily Mail*, most popular of the cheap dailies, remembered that it was during these years that:

> We realized that one of the greatest forces, almost untapped, at the disposal of the Press was the depth and volume of public interest in Imperial questions. We never allowed the peoples at home to forget the magnificent heritage they enjoyed through the valiancy and self-sacrifice of their fathers.[57]

However, the process of imperial interpellation began even earlier than contact with newspapers. H.O. Arnold-Forster's *Citizen-Reader: For the Use of Schools* invited children to:

> Look at the map in front of this book and think what is meant by all those red patches which you will see dotted over every part of it. . . . And all of you ought to remember that the great nation to which you will belong, and of which, I hope, you are all proud is bigger far bigger than the three little islands which make-up the kingdom of Great Britain and Ireland.[58]

Pride that it was the energy of the race that had given the British their Empire was to be heard also in Sir Walter Besant's *The Rise of Empire*, published just a few months after *The Seven Seas*. It had as its paramount concern the vital necessity of a general awareness of the significance of empire, and it called 'upon my readers to learn how the existence of the mighty Empire affects each one personally'.[59] Three years later, defending *The Seven Seas* against Buchanan's condemnation of it as an excrescence of 'Hooliganism', Besant claimed that, on the contrary, through it Kipling:

> . . . has brought home to the understanding of the most parochial of Little Englanders the sense and knowledge of what the British Empire means. What Seeley taught scholars, Kipling has taught the multitude. He is the poet of the Empire. Not the jingo-rhymer; the poet with the deepest reverence for those who have built up the Empire . . .[60]

Reading these sentiments now it is not difficult to understand why J.A. Hobson feared that the newly literate British public was peculiarly vulnerable to such propaganda. 'Popular education', he declared, 'instead of serving as a defence is an incitement towards imperialism: it has opened up a panorama of vulgar pride and crude sensationalism to a great inert mass who see current history and the tangled maze of world movements with dim, bewildered eyes.'[61] While the work of Richard Price has suggested that jingoism was the prerogative of the lower middle class, produced by what he calls their 'status anxiety', various memoirs and research by, for example, historians of the music hall, have shown that the working class are not to be absolved entirely from imperial enthusiasms.[62]

Hyndman, founder of the Social Democratic Federation, noted the extraordinarily jingoistic behaviour of the lower end of the London poor in his *Reminiscences* and speculated in 1900 that this wave of imperialism had prevented the occurrence of class war.[63] In a similar vein, Robert Roberts has described the pervasive nature of imperial and patriotic ideas and pageantry and the publications, advertisements and ephemera through which they were expressed.[64] This impression is also confirmed by oral evidence. Stephen Humphries notes in his collection that 'the ideology of imperialism made a direct appeal to working-class youth because it reflected and reinforced a number of its cultural traditions, in particular the street gangs' concern with territorial rivalry, and the assertion of masculinity'.[65] Several of the new *Barrack-Room Ballads* showed an awareness of working-class morals and attitudes, and they made deliberate use of them in an effort to arouse a socially diverse imperial enthusiasm that would incorporate those on whose military service the Empire was dependent.

Besides 'Soldier & Sailor Too' and 'Sappers', which praised the men of two regiments in particular for extending the Empire, several of the ballads equated imperial adventure and attitudes with the essence of masculinity. In 'The Ladies', for example, imperial aggression is an opportunity to ' 've 'ad my pickin' o' sweet'earts', in the course of which all women are debased in a racist order, so that 'the things you will learn from the Yellow an' Brown, / They'll 'elp you a lot with the White!'[66] Another ballad, 'Mary, Pity Women!', often presented as a sympathetic portrayal of the lot of the working-class girl, who continues to love her man, even when he deserts her when she is with child, in fact promotes an image of women as unable to be anything other than stupid and emotional. Although 'the mother that bore you . . . knew it all before you', the forsaken woman still cries 'Ah, Gawd, I love you so![67] The men in these poems, like the pioneers in 'The Song of the English', are the active agents, always in control of their own fate and the fate of others and their brutal machismo increases their stature.

Just as the *Departmental Ditties* were sung all over British India, so it seems that these new ballads enjoyed the same popular remit. One of Kipling's reviewers reported that the new *Barrack-Room Ballads*, 'set to old tunes are already sung wherever the British soldier plants his camp', and he added that the correspondent of the *Times*, who had been with the recent expedition to Dongola, had reported that, while he sat writing, the soldiers outside his tent were singing one of Kipling's songs.[68] It is reasonable to assume, therefore, that these ballads played a part in bringing imperial awareness to working people via their own 'native' traditions. When we remember that the music hall at this time had many acts that made use of an imperial context, it seems to indicate at least a willingness on the part of the working classes to be drawn into a sense of national superiority and complicity in the maintenance of imperial enterprise. It might be argued that capital investment largely determined the content of the halls, but this does not explain the popularity of songs like Charles Godfrey's 'It's the English-Speaking Race against the World' and 'Sons of the Sea', written especially for the Diamond Jubilee.[69]

There is much in fact to suggest that all classes were imbued with this sense of national superiority that taught the colonized world that it was fortunate to come under English suzerainty. At times, Joseph Chamberlain buttressed his presentation of empire as a good business proposition, with the claim that 'the British race is the greatest of governing races that the world has ever seen' and it was, therefore, incumbent upon it 'to fulfil the mission which our history and our national character have imposed upon us'.[70] Indeed, imperialism broke the mould of Victorian politics as many even of the Liberal leaders conceded its first principle. Lord Rosebery declared unequivocally in 1900 that, 'An empire such as ours requires as its first condition an imperial race – a race vigorous and industrious and intrepid.'[71]

The similarities it has been possible to observe here between different social and political discourses confirms Tony Bennett's characterization of culture as an area of exchange between the ideologies of the dominant and subordinate classes. However, it is important to understand that this exchange was a process working within the dominant consensus and various institutions, among them literary criticism, policed this exchange to ensure that the boundaries of class culture were not contested. However, it remains to be emphasized that the national pride and imperial enthusiasm bred by *The Seven Seas* and the multiplicity of discourses that surrounded it were dependent upon the notion of 'lesser breeds'.[72] Edward Said has aptly described the way in which:

> . . . distant hegemony over non-white peoples . . . [was] inscribed by right in the very fabric of European and Western Christian society, whether that society was liberal, monarchical or revolutionary. . . . At the heart of European culture during the many decades of imperial expansion lay what could be called an undeterred and unrelenting Eurocentrism. This accumulated experiences, territories, peoples, histories, it studied them, it classified them, it verified them; but above all it subordinated them to the culture and indeed the very idea of white Christian Europe.[73]

The Seven Seas assumed such an hierarchy of races. Take the 'Dedication' in which the speaker reflects that:

> So I thank God my birth
> Fell not in isles aside –
> Waste headlands of the earth,
> Or warring tribes untried –
> But that she lent me worth
> And gave me right to pride,[74]

The colonial racism expressed here turned on the recognition of racial, cultural and historical differences. It rendered the native culture uninhabitable by invalidating its entire way of life. Later there was the certainty that:

> Surely in toil or fray
> Under an alien sky,
> Comfort it is to say;
> 'Of no mean city am I![75]

In these lines also from the 'Dedication', as in those other examples from different discourses, the subjugated people were considered to be 'naturally subservient to a superior, advanced, developed and morally-mature' English imperial race whose 'doom and pride' it was to rule, instruct, legislate, develop, and at the proper times, to discipline, and, as the occasion served, remove the troublesome – as we saw earlier in those lines that gave the imperialist the order to:[76]

> Keep ye the Law . . .
> Clear the land of evil . . .
> Make ye sure to each his own
> . . .
> By the peace among Our peoples let men know
> we serve the Lord![77]

The degeneracy of the colonized justified conquest and demanded the establishment of institutions and systems of administration. The extension of such institutions around the world was, inevitably, based upon territorial acquisition and aggression. 'The Lost Legion' speaks with pride about how 'We've painted The Islands vermilion', and 'The Native Born' sees the Empire growing as it raises a toast to:

> To the last and the largest Empire,
> To the map that is half unrolled![78]

The assumption here that England would soon dominate the world was an assumption too that empires were the thing of the future, that very soon there would be no place in the world that was not part of one. It has been calculated that between 1876 and 1915, one-quarter of the globe was distributed and redistributed as colonies among half a dozen states and Britain took the largest proportion of this land. It may be misleading, therefore, to suggest, as Bernard Porter does, that the 'visionary' imperialists played no forward role in this expansion and 'only completed the building, most of whose fabric had risen before them'.[79] This was certainly not the impression of contemporary observers. The critic Robert Buchanan, a disgruntled Gladstonian Liberal, remarked that:

> . . . we have exhibited lately, in our dealings with other nationalities, a greed of gain, a vainglory, a cruelty, and a boastful indifference to the rights of others, of which in days when the old philanthropic spirit was abroad we should simply have been incapable.[80]

The ambiguous role of the new imperialists is, perhaps, typified in the confusion that still remains about Chamberlain's part in the Jameson Raid. Kipling's poem 'Hymn Before Action', written and published in *The Times* during it, suggests that this group were making vigorous efforts either to justify or to conceal acquisitive motives beneath a cloud of righteousness.[81]

The 'Hymn Before Action' presents the Raid as a crusade of the godly. By the end of the poem, just before the battle begins, the English were described in terms of a chosen people, 'Fulfilled of signs and wonders', 'Jehovah of the Thunders' was on their side, the 'heathen', who knelt 'At Altars not Thine own', received prayers of intercession, while the enemy in its 'panic, pride and Terror' neatly became everything that the noble British were not. Those who represented English imperial interest were in other words transformed into a band of Christian soldiers, who sought only to rid the country of a brutal enemy that would extort 'Revenge that knows no rein'. The poetic manoeuvre was neither original nor complicated, the enemy was debased, while the English were justified by their Christian humility, typified by the final sentiments of the army before battle, as it prayed not for itself, but for 'True comrade and true foeman'.[82]

However, poetic glorification and justification was the only kind that the English received over this affair. The Raid produced a wave of anti-British feeling, symbolized in the famous telegram from the Kaiser that congratulated Kruger on his repulse of Jameson. Liberal opinion in England was outraged by what it saw as 'the Hooligan spirit of patriotism', transparently aggressive action motivated solely by greed for territory and desire for national supremacy.[83] Both Chamberlain and Rhodes had to appear before a Commission of Enquiry to explain themselves and, although the Colonial Secretary was exonerated, the whole affair seemed to indicate that 'the Power with the Need' thoroughly controlled and determined the more visionary motivations of the 'missionaries of empire'. In the 'Hymn Before Action', only through the use and abuse of Christian precept had it been possible to mystify the situation acknowledged at the outset, that the interests of the English could only be furthered by gaining advantages over other nation-states. Struggle was necessary to survival and to establish superiority:

> The Nations in their harness
> Go up against our path.[84]

Similarly, in 'The Song of the English' the 'Power with the Need' of empire had brought moments that acknowledged that the crucial reality was a world in which 'The Cities are full of Pride / Challenging each to each'.[85] Although profit, privilege and usurpation were not allowed to tarnish this version of English national identity, they were only displaced, they were revealed as endemic in the places established by the imperial race. In 'The Song of the Cities', aggression and gross commercialism were the key to their existence past and present: from Hong Kong 'sweeps / Thy warships down the bay!', Capetown stood revealed as 'Snatched and bartered oft from hand to hand' and in Hobart 'man's hate made me Hell'.[86]

Although in the first part of the collection the 'Vision' received both the largest and, as one critic observed, the loudest place, there were points where it was compromised by the 'Power with the Need' and revealed as no more than realpolitik.[87] This occurred particularly when the verse attended to the economic and political determinations that stood at the centre of the imperial enterprise. Just as many of the poems in *Departmental Ditties & Other Verses* had been produced by the conviction that in important respects the Indian Empire was under threat, so the balance between 'the Vision . . . with the Power & the Need' was at its most precarious when incidents such as the Jameson Raid made the sense of being endangered by enemies acute.

The second set of *Barrack-Room Ballads*, which concentrated its attention on 'drafs from Gawd knows where', take on their meaning in relation to the commitment to achieve an imperial enthusiasm, the conviction of racial superiority and the growing feeling that the Empire was besieged.[88] This group of poems, like the first collection of that name, did however disturb reviewers. They wondered why an author inspired as he was by 'idealism' in 'The Song of the English' should have 'given us the squalid side of the British soldier or sailor' and have so 'exaggerated the evil of the world'.[89] They were it seems offended that *The Seven Seas* should have included individuals and types, who, in their behaviour, manner and attitudes appeared, in the view of these representatives of the governing and propertied classes, to threaten and disrupt the very qualities of character and social values so emphatically asserted in the first part of the collection. Their reactions certainly bore a resemblance to those which had greeted the first volume of that name and were indicative of the paradoxical situation that the 'visionary imperialists' were in when they tried to promote their ideas in the England of the 1890s.

They recognized that if a world empire of the sort they imagined were to come into existence, it would require an imperial enthusiasm that was not merely an aquiescence in the mere maintenance of the Empire. A discourse was needed that would incorporate the masses and create some semblance of unity across class and party lines. This, however, was a particularly difficult task at a time when the extension of the franchise again was arousing the fear that social mass was about to be transmuted into political class. Any attempt to create an imperial enthusiasm that went beyond a commonality of interests and brought classes closer to one another was regarded with extreme distaste. This period was conceived by many of the ruling class as a battle against socialism; thus, the Archbishop of Canterbury, E.W. Benson, noted after the

Diamond Jubilee that 'days afterwards, everyone feels that the socialist movement has had a check'.[90] Clearly, the sense of national superiority encouraged by such occasions, the cross-class complicity in the maintenance of imperial supremacy, did not extend to a desire for any changes in the metropolitan status quo. In 1885, when Joseph Chamberlain had launched his 'unauthorized programme' at a working-men's demonstration, and asked 'What ransom will property pay for the security it enjoys?', he had been denounced as 'the advocate of blackmail, confiscation, plunder and communism'.[91] Any effort to suggest that an imperial outlook might alter class relations in the metropolitan merely brought to the surface the class tensions that divided metropolitan society.

The reviewers who discussed the second collection of *Barrack-Room Ballads* were disturbed by the illustrations in this volume of a discourse that sought to promote a notion of social inclusiveness which would have provided the metropolitan basis for a world empire. The *Quarterly Review* was representative in discovering in the ballads only 'a coarse pulse of feeling'.[92] Yet a variety of means had been employed to suggest that in the imperial outlook, social intercourse would be diversified and class divisions might in some instances be laid aside. There was, for example, the inclusion of the voices of working or self-made men in *The Seven Seas* part of the collection. Speaking without the sophistications of traditional poetic rhetoric or education, these men were, nevertheless, to be heard articulating middle-class values and the most laudable sentiments. 'Mc Andrew's Hymn' ended on a note of Calvinistic asceticism, with a peroration to 'Law, Orrder, Duty an' Restraint, Obedience, Discipline' as the qualities that would, with the aid of the machine, help run and extend the Empire.[93] Even the less respectable 'merchant prince' in 'The Mary Gloster' only revealed his peccadilloes on his death-bed, having through life been guided by the sound entrepreneurial principle that 'It all comes back to the business'.[94] More overtly, 'The Song of the Banjo' revealed the coming together, 'link by link', in the imperial adventure of both dominant and subordinate classes. This 'war-drum of the White Man round the world!', that played 'the Song of Roland' and the 'Common tunes that make you choke and blow your nose', drew on that common reservoir of feeling that united 'the Younger Son . . . the rearguard . . . Johnny Bowlegs' and 'all that ever went with evening dress'. This was effected by means of common feeling and incorporation of social groups that drew 'the world together . . . from Delos up to Limerick and back!'[95]

Perhaps the greatest effort to submerge the differences between discursive formations occurred through the poetic voices that closed and opened both sections of the collection. The emphasis on a common response and outlook to the adventure and fulfilment that empire offered emerged very obviously in the deliberate patterning of the 'Sestina of the Tramp-Royal' and 'For to Admire', the concluding poems of the two sections in the volume. The imperial urge to be about 'The 'appy roads that take you oe'r the world' has been the prime motivation of both speakers, the thing that has given meaning to their lives.[96] *The Seven Seas* ends on this note:

> Gawd bless this world! Whatever she 'ath done
> Excep' when awful long – I've found it good.
> So write, before I die, 'E liked it all![97]

Barrack-Room Ballads closes in a similarly effusive manner, that in the satisfaction it expresses is a spur to others to try this lifestyle:

> *For to admire an' for to see,*
> *For to be'old this world so wide –*
> *It never done no good to me,*
> *But I can't drop it if I tried!*[98]

The admitted hardships increased the stature of the speakers and advertised the imperial outlook as one that was nationally enhancing.

The parallels were there also between the 'Dedication' and 'When' 'Omer smote 'is bloomin' lyre'. Both worked within a remit that admitted only those things which bound their readers together. The 'Dedication' spoke of a unity of loyalty and nationalism. In 'stranger lands', the English clung to their own 'isles', 'As a child to a mother's gown', and among 'Waste headlands of the earth / Or warring tribes untried', they were assured that their 'right to pride' placed them among the blessed. The opening of the *Barrack-Room Ballads* claimed the same ground as the 'Dedication', with the assertion that the soldier voice sang the same song as ' 'Omer'. High and low were one, they both dealt in 'old songs' that 'turn-up again'. Rhetorical differences were a superficiality, as 'you. . . . The market-girls an' fisherman / The shepherds an' the sailors, too' knew only too well. All discourse was one discourse so that ' 'Omer', the symbol of high discourse, might wink back at the soldier, secure in the knowledge that they understood one another. In revealing the common ground between high and low, the poems transgressed the rules of hierarchy and social order.[99]

The same effect was sought in 'The Mother Lodge', which through a Masonic example showed that the imperial framework was able to include all sorts and conditions of men in a way that offered no threat to the existing social structure – all the 'common man' was offered was good fellowship. Over a 'smoke', men from different social positions met tolerantly, ideas and differences could be exchanged, understanding would emerge and, having in this way 'met on the Level', men would happily return to their proper stations in life – 'Station Master, Railman, servant of the Commissariat and Conductor-Sargent'. Significantly, however, this levelling occurred in the outer reaches of the Empire and the response to it in an English context was likely to have been less than sanguine. As well as being a period when the working classes enjoyed imperial pageantry and supported the maintenance of empire, it was also one of renewed trade union activity, when relations between employers and employed became increasingly bitter. There would have been those who found it hard to imagine a situation in which 'Inside' men might call one another 'Brother', while 'Outside' as they parted company rank would be restored 'Sergeant! Sir! Salute! Salaam!.'[100]

Richard Shannon has typified this decade domestically as one in which there was a 'new working-class consciousness of possibilities' and although 'The Shut-Eye Sentry' bespoke the devotion of men for their officers it must have drawn a wry smile from those living through the 1890s in England.[101] The rankers of the ballad were so loyal to their officer that after a drunken debauch on his part:

> We sluiced 'im down an' we washed 'im out,
> An' a first-class job we made,
> When we saved 'im smart as a bombardier,
> For six o'clock parade.[102]

Their sole purpose in these actions it seems was to maintain the existing military order and reputation of their regiment. However, to those not so confident of the desire of the working classes to keep in place the existing status quo, the final comment in the ballad might have appeared to have the knowingness of the potential blackmailer: '*We'll 'elp 'im for 'is mother, an' 'e'll 'elp us by-an-by*!'[103]

Perhaps, it was 'The 'Eathen', however, that was the least likely to have made the political point it intended and aroused instead the most disturbing reflections.[104] The 1890s had seen the publication of what became known as slumming reports, which exposed the submerged tenth of English society. Unemployed and living in the most degraded conditions these people were seen by the other classes as indigent and without any interest or part in existing society to which they therefore represented a threat. *In Darkest England*, published in 1890, compared what many of the propertied classes saw as the detritus of society to what they imagined to be the brutish uncivilized natives that peopled the Empire. Both the reports and Kipling's poem reinforce once more the connection Benedict Anderson posits between class ideologies and racism, as well as, of course, reinscribing the essential inferiority of 'natives' and constituting them as everything that was other to 'civilized' expectations.[105] The deliberate analogy in 'The 'Eathen' between the new recruit and the 'native' must have released in many readers the fears that surrounded it. The ballad suggested that the new recruit, drawn from the lowest social regions, hailing from 'Gawd knows where', was, on his arrival in the Army, just like 'The 'eathen in 'is blindness' who 'don't obey no orders unless they is 'is own', who 'keeps 'is side-arms awful' and who is, generally:

All along o' dirtiness, all along o' mess,
All along o' doin' things rather more or less.[106]

The degree of 'Johnny Raw's' degradation was meant to accentuate the power of transformation the Army was able to exert. After he had been 'licked into shape' he took pride in himself and in his appearance, he obeyed orders and, most importantly, he had 'the Core at 'eart'.[107] His initial selfish individualism was replaced by a notion of transcendence, of the existence and importance of a whole larger than himself to which he would willingly sacrifice even his own life. However, while there might have been those who were willing to credit that the Army could work this effect, there must have been others, like the reviewer Robert Buchanan, who noted that 'Tommy Atkins' was essentially a 'Hooligan', and who realized that at any time the Army depended on those who were, or had been, the dregs of society and who in any period of civil disorder would be a volatile commodity – 'What security for the stormy times to come?' did such a military offer.[108]

'Back to the Army Again' was another ballad that drew issues such as these into sharp focus, thereby compromising the ideal of an imperial ideology that was socially inclusive. It dealt with the Army's recruitment problems and how these might be alleviated if it could re-enlist men who had already served with the Colours but were now in the Reserve. Such a system had been instituted by the Cardwell reforms. The ballad suggested that if men were able to re-enlist, many of those who roamed the streets would have been able to come in 'out o' the cold and rain' and 'A man o' four-and-twenty who hasn't learned of a trade' would find the employment society was unable to offer him.[109] Both the Army and the social fabric would be improved by such men rejoining their regiments. But, again, in the course of the poem, the English readers either became aware of or were reminded of the existence of groups from whom they felt a great distance and whom they feared. It did not take a genius to work out that the ongoing problem of the Army in this instance left the potentiality for disorder and the threat to property within civil society. Incorporated within the Army, or, because of legislation, excluded from it, the men on which it depended signified some of the deepest divisions within English society during this period.

Ironically, therefore, these ballads that tried to persuade their readers of a commonality of interests between classes or tried to provide solutions to socially threatening situations were in fact the ones that highlighted class tension and acute social problems. *Barrack-Room Ballads*, like some of the poems in *The Seven Seas*, failed to sustain the 'Vision', or, their assertions existed in direct contradiction to the forces and circumstances prevalent in English society at this time. The return offered to the working classes on this socially inclusive discourse was a reinscription of existing traditions and good fellowship bred in the distance of the Empire. If the response of the reviewers was representative, probably all the ruling groups found there was a reminder of some of their worst fears. The threat Kipling represented to both literary and class interests was typified in the now famous review of his work by Robert Buchanan that was published in 1899.[110]

The review was a long one that began by noting the entry onto the political stage of the masses which had brought 'a back-wave of barbarism', characterized by 'the universal scramble for plunder . . . the worship of physical force and commercial success in any and every form' over which 'the flag of a Hooligan imperialism is raised'. Those who ruled the country merely sought the approval of the 'clamorous appeal' of the masses. The centrepiece of the review was, however, an attack on Kipling's popularity with that 'modern monstrosity, the conservative working man, who exchanges his birthright of freedom and free thought for . . . the platitudes of cockney patriotism'.[111] Clearly, Buchanan, like many others, especially among the older Liberals, feared a future shaped by Tory populism, of the sort recently exhibited by Randolph Churchill in his courting of the working man. Aided by the newspaper press, that 'mighty engine' for 'keeping the public intelligence on a low level', the masses would be manipulated to suit the interests of the wealthy classes. In the face of this, the 'sober and self-respecting human beings' of the past, 'noble and magnanimous', would disappear in the future. Here was an elegy for what was seen to be the demise of the liberal middle classes and what Buchanan saw as their essentially humane and Christian values. They had been replaced, he argued, by the new imperialism which was no more than 'the worship of physical force and commercial success' borne out in the recent Jameson Raid and by a poem like the 'Hymn to Action'. He described the Army as it appeared in the ballads as 'just drunk, bragging, boasting Hooligans in red coats' and one hears the same note of fear that had initially greeted the arrival of 'Tommy Atkins'.[112] However, the source of his literary and political anger and fear comes in the following passage in which, on the subject of Kipling's work, he reflects that:

> The truth is . . . these lamentable productions were concocted not for sane men or self-respecting soldiers . . . but for the "mean whites" of our eastern civilization, the idle and loafing men in the street, and for such women, the well-dressed Doll Tearsheets of cities, as shriek at their heels. Mr Kipling's vocabulary is a purely cockney vocabulary . . . familiar enough in Seven Dials. . . . Turning over the leaves of his poems, one is transported at once to the region of low-drinking dens and gin palaces, of dirty dissipation and drunken brawls.[113]

No passage could show more clearly how the literary institution was at this time imbricated in other regions of ideological struggle: the class tension within literary and imperial discourses is clearly evident here. The ' "mean whites" of our eastern civilization', inhabitants of London's East End, were safer ruled and subordinated as the 'natives' were in the Empire. Once they were addressed, a process of incorporation had begun which had the same kind of uncomfortable implications for the literary world as the extension of the franchise had for the political. Cockney dialect, realism constituted by 'gin palaces of dirty dissipation', the transference of Shakespeare's characters from the literary pantheon back to the streets whence they came, started a reversal of dominant literary values and called into question contemporary critical judgement. Kipling's 'almost unexampled popularity' was another example, like the publications of Newnes and Pearson, that offered at this time to convert a reading public of specialist groups into a mass readership which might eventually challenge the liberal consensus of the existing literary institution. The political need to secure the working-class vote had been recognized recently by the Conservative Party; now a writer who made no secret of his support for it emerged who, the evidence suggested, managed to reach the mass of readers. The old Tory warhorse, *Blackwood's*, was, of course, delighted with this achievement: 'It has been Mr Kipling's enviable task to bring patriotism from the closet to the street, and to diffuse its benificent influence among millions who had hitherto remained untouched.'[114]

The literary reviewers had, from the outset, been more hesitant about this achievement and, by the end of the century, as Buchanan's review showed, the popular success of the verse became an important reason behind its failure with many critics. The reviewing institution then – as now – defined popular literature as that which was characterized by its numerical appeal, but also by its lack of value as determined by their own critical standards. A populist writer able to appeal across class lines, in the same volume, by making use of both dominant and popular discourses, was the greatest threat of all because in the same space he exposed the class tension at the heart of literary definitions.

The Seven Seas was, therefore, a crucial volume that had a decisive effect on Kipling's literary reputation and on the development of his political outlook. Relations with the literary establishment that were produced by the threat that he appeared to pose to the social hierarchy and to literary definitions continued to influence his reception by it throughout his life. The collapse of the possibility of federation, the failure to take hold of the kind of imperial enthusiasm that he envisioned and the fading of the dream of world empire, all increased the fear on which these dreams had been built and sharpened it in the future.

FOUR

'Before a Midnight Breaks in Storm'

The Five Nations 1903

In a victory ceremony during the Boer War, outside the Volksrad, the Parliament of the Transvaal, 10,000 British soldiers sang Kipling's 'Recessional'.[1] The acclaim it had received on its publication in *The Times* in 1897 was extended and confirmed in the years that followed by its reappearance in many authorized and unauthorized versions; and the use made of it in South Africa clearly suggests that, by 1900, it had sufficiently permeated the Army for it to have accompanied it on a campaign thousands of miles away from England. Its sentiments and its appeal to the 'Lord God of Hosts' were deemed, it would appear, to be those most appropriate to this particular series of English triumphs during the Boer War. A year later, reflecting on 'The Poetry of Mr Kipling', Edward Dowden commented that, 'It was long since a morsel of verse constituted an historical event of importance for two hemispheres; but this without exaggeration, is what certain short poems of Kipling have been.' This writer had become 'a maker of tribal lays', able to anticipate the national mood and to assist in the outbreak and shaping of that mood.[2] Many of the poems to which Dowden was referring came from *The Five Nations*, having first appeared in newspapers as diverse as *The Times* and the *Daily Mail*. It was also during the period covered by this volume that Kipling wrote 'The Absent-Minded Beggar', which even in today's terms might be described as a media event of significant proportions, being sung in music halls, recited in theatres and parlours to raise money for disabled soldiers, orphans and widows that the Boer War would shortly produce.

Such evidence would indicate that Kipling's verse was capable of the same kind of popular remit that in its first appearances had allowed it to spread like wildfire through the different levels of Anglo-Indian society and which had, as we have seen, proved so disturbing for the literary institution in England. As a political poet he was, as he quite deliberately set out to be, a force with which to be reckoned. When *The Times* received from Kipling a poem with the note that he required no payment, it was understood that in his view he was speaking on an issue of national importance and an editorial on the same subject usually followed. No other political poet has ever had either the means, or sufficient reputation, to appeal to the nation in this way. Neither, as a result of such means and reputation, has any other political poet been able to achieve entry into so many groups across the social formation as a whole. *The Five Nations*, more perhaps than the other collections, makes it quite clear why Kipling pursued his role as a political poet in such a consistent and unswerving manner.

The lines he had written shortly after he returned from India showed that Kipling understood that with the extension of democracy the support of the electorate as a whole for imperial policy was increasingly important.[3] A felt collectivity is always a crucial prerequisite for successful political action, and in the 1890s this meant that the good opinion of the electorate was essential for the successful prosecution of overseas interests. Public opinion defined in this way was the only sure foundation for governmental policy. Gladstone had shown how foreign affairs could enthuse the masses; Kipling, on the other side of the political divide and a fervent imperialist, saw that the real problem was the creation of sound views about the Empire that would ensure its growing strength and continuance, for unlike Gladstone, he was not convinced that either the masses or the classes possessed at moments of imperial crisis an instinctive righteousness. Indeed, he feared that 'the only serious enemy to Empire, within or without, is that very Democracy which depends on the Empire for its proper comforts'.[4] This in no way ran contrary to his faith in the qualities of those who rode in the 'third-class carriages'.[5] It was democratic forms that he detested, the frequent changes of government that brought changes in imperial policy that destroyed its coherence and consistency and, therefore, its power.

To those concerned as he was about the future of the Empire, outbursts of public feeling were a menace because of their irrationality. The vacillation of the recently enfranchised was to be feared, just as was the rush and gush of upper-class London. The work of Koebner and Schmidt shows quite clearly the changes over a short period to the meaning attached by the public to the term 'imperialism'.[6] Neither the public nor the opinion of public opinion were fixed categories. And, when Britain stood challenged at every turn by Germany, Russia and France, and this occurred more than once during the period in which the verses in *The Five Nations* were written, imperialists saw the fluctuations in public opinion as the surest way to ruin. *The Seven Seas* had shown that Kipling was aware of the great pool of sentiment that could be attached to empire and he had sought to harness it. His poetry in that volume stemmed from the notion that it was a site where forms of consciousness and identity might be constituted. The verses in *The Five Nations* were another attempt to inform and by doing so transform public opinion, though in this collection celebratory verses had almost disappeared and they did not mediate, as they had tended to do in *The Seven Seas*, the general impression that the world in which the British Empire existed was a powerful and hostile one. The stimulus to these collections was the same as that behind the earlier two and it was the single most important motivation behind all Kipling's political poetry: the absence of what he deemed to be sound views in the nation when and where they were required about the Empire.

In a now much quoted passage, the Italian Marxist Gramsci spelt out his prescription for the 'new intellectual', who, at a time of crisis, could contribute to the making of collective consciousness:

> The mode of being of the new intellectual can no longer consist in eloquence, which is an exterior and momentary mover of feelings and passions, but in active participation in pratical life, as constructor organiser, "permanent persuader" and not just a simple orator.[7]

The activities of Kipling that accompanied his verse in the years covered by this volume suggests that his impassioned commitment to the imperial ideal caused him to fulfil the kind of role Gramsci spoke about. Turning down a knighthood at the outset of the Boer War, he thoroughly involved himself in a whole range of small and larger activities connected with it, which reinforced his poetic press statements: from the organization of village rifle clubs and the distribution of pyjamas to the troops, through to public speeches about South Africa and an active participation in a pamphlet campaign to promote the war. He became, along with Chamberlain, the figure most hated by the pro-Boers. In Gramscian terms, Kipling's activities ensured that his verse became ' "directive" [specialised and political]'.[8]

Not surprisingly, therefore, while it is indisputable that during these years the publicity that Kipling's verse received made it available to an enormously wide range of people, there is also evidence that, despite its spectacular successes, by 1903 it held less favour than it had, and that its outreach was in fact contracting. *The Seven Seas* went through three editions in the first 4 months of its publication; however, it was 6 years before *The Five Nations* had run through five editions. The enthusiastic response to certain poems, published in newspapers, was, therefore, paralleled by a noticeable decline in the sales of his books. Something had occurred, it would seem, that deterred the book-buying public from purchasing so many of his poetic wares. This was the start of the phase in which this group of readers began to show with their pockets the reservations about the writer that the reviewers of his poetry had shown from the outset.

The reasons for this relative decline are rather more, perhaps, than his 'very muddled' political thinking, for both political parties and their leaders were guilty of this then as now; neither can it be put down entirely to his mind being shrouded by 'an iron curtain or political dogma', because it had been in this state from the outset and would be so to the finish.[9] No writer of equal imaginative power ever spoke out more consistently in support of a political ideal. Rather, it would seem that his reputation faltered at this time, because, in pursuit of his ideal of an England bound together by patriotic service, in fear and trepidation that the Empire would be lost, he intentionally specified the ground of his attack and included in it social groups and institutions that had previously escaped his satire. In this process, of course, he offended many who might previously have felt attuned to his views. The second and more fundamental reason for the change in Kipling's popularity arose from the conflicting attitudes towards imperialism reactivated and brought into fierce debate by the Boer War. It served as a rallying point for a vociferous anti-imperialist movement that, ultimately, served as the most effective antidote to the imperial fever that burned in Britain on occasions like the 1897 Jubilee and with which, as we saw, Kipling was associated, although he deemed his Imperium as quite different.

The Boer War revealed the weakness and inefficiency of the metropolitan and the event seemed to cast uncertainty on the imperial future. The consequent mood of dismay had been reinforced by the meditations stimulated by the old Queen's death and the turn of the century, with its stark evidence of the increasing might, in every sense, of the USA and Germany. The attempts to rearrange political ideas and actions in accordance with such realizations and the simultaneous adjustments in national self-awareness also served to reposition Kipling's writing in relation to its various publics.

A reader now encountering the poems in *The Five Nations* for the first time might not find it easy to understand the purpose behind the arrangement of the verse in this volume. It follows no chronological order, verse written in 1896 has been sandwiched between that produced in 1902, and there is even one poem written as far back as 1892. The sea poems with which the volume begin soon tail off and the collection lacks, at first sight, the consistency of theme and the deliberate arrangement that had gone into *Barrack-Room Ballads* and which was even clearer in *The Seven Seas*. Once, however, the chronology of the poems contained in the volume is recovered, some of the reasons for the thematic and temporal disarray become apparent. Seventy per cent of the verses in this collection were written between 1900 and 1903, that is during and after the Boer War. One of the reasons for the dispersal of these poems throughout the collection is partly to be explained by Kipling's acute business acumen. He could not have been unaware that the book-buying public would be less than enthusiastic about any work that consistently and substantially addressed itself to the recent war. As he had said in 'The Lesson', any reflection on that event was more than a little discomforting. After September 1900, when Kruger fled to Europe, the pressmen noted how public interest in the war decreased rapidly. The pro-Boers continued their campaign and their protests were swelled by soldiers sending home letters that complained about the conduct of the war. All of these were factors that would have suggested to a writer wishing to maximize the sale of his work that any obvious concentration on the subject of the Boer War in 1903 would not be a lucrative strategy. It was an instance where even the mightily committed political poet had to pay some attention to the need of the professional writer to make his living and maintain at least some of his popular remit.

It seems unlikely, however, that the dispersal of later poems throughout the collection was due to sales considerations alone. Indeed, it is likely from what we know about the care with which Kipling normally constructed his verse collections, that the placing of poems without respect to chronology was deliberate: it became a means of directing the readers' attention towards what he deemed to be 'real issues'. Early in the collection, after several verses which dealt with naval life and ships of war, whose 'office' was to guide 'the foe to their doom', Kipling confronted his readers with an indictment of a generation that had gone 'too far from the beach . . . to know how the outworks stand' and brought disaster upon itself.[10] This indictment was written 3 years after the opening poems. Repeatedly throughout the collection, later verses written during the Boer War were given this kind of commentary status. At the time, this connection between the verses must have been understood by some, as it was intended to be, as recriminatory. Others more charitably disposed towards the poet might have felt that the dispersal throughout the collection of his estimations of the state of the nation, and its unwillingness to shoulder its imperial destiny, pointed to his insight – that from early on he understood what was at stake. Kipling to such readers became the inspired prophet, the Cassandra who had warned of impending disaster over an extended period, one of those who understood that power was built on efficiency and strength. The evidence suggests, however, that by 1903 there were fewer such readers about. In both of the modern anthologies of Kipling's verse, the most vituperative of the work that he wrote during these years, which did much to damage his reputation, is included, which suggests either that the English are a nation not afraid to acknowledge their own weaknesses, or that some would wish them to be still reminded of them. Neither implication would have pleased the author of these very powerful invectives.

The brief span in years covered by *The Five Nations* was one, therefore, in which there had been significant changes. Empire enthusiasm had reached a zenith from whence it had commanded the support of both political parties. However, these years also included the shattering of this confidence by the Boer War which, once again, split politicians and nation in their attitude towards the Empire and the role they foresaw for themselves in history. Some of the poems included in *The Five Nations*, however, dated from 1895, when Kipling was still living in the USA, and like 'The Song of the English' they present an imperialism couched in religious terms and expressed with all the fervour of a true believer. Imperialism is here a form of Calvinism, 'The Explorer' appears as a figure chosen by God and guided by:

> . . . one everlasting Whisper day and night repeated – so: "Something hidden. Go and find it. Go and look behind the Ranges – Something lost behind the Ranges. Lost and waiting for you, Go!"[11]

None who follows him are his equal, though they 'take the credit' and 'go up and occupy'.[12] The imperialist of this poem and those of 'The Feet of the Young Men' are aggressively masculine and the language is that of force, power and struggle.[13] They find their place in history and with God through their selfless spirit of adventure and the kind of sacrifice and suffering it imposes on them. Imperial activity is formulated in a way that is calculated to encourage readers to link the fate of the Empire with their own belief in the worth of individual initiative and this was an approach that might compel the allegiance of the middle classes. It was one that Disraeli had used before and to the same purpose because he, like Kipling, 'endeavoured to develop and strengthen our Empire, believing that the combination of achievement and responsibility elevates the character and condition of a people'.[14] This notion had received loud expression in 'The Flag of England' in Kipling's first volume of collected verse, which had warned that the only way that the English could escape provincialism and assume the role for which history had chosen them was by expanding their Empire. Lord Lugard had expressed the idea with greater brevity when he said that '. . . a nation, like an individual, must have some task higher than the pursuit of material gain, if it is to escape the benumbing influence of parochialism and to fulfil its higher destiny'.[15]

Verses such as these in the *Five Nations* placed Kipling within the mainstream of Conservative thought as one of the many who, at this time, insisted upon the ethical significance of conquest. More importantly, perhaps, they contributed to that disturbance in Liberal thinking which occurred during this period. The essence of the imperialism on offer here was that, despite its romantic and redemptive appeal to the individual, its interest was essentially collectivist: it was organized around corporate rather than individual interests, it claimed to represent the organic interests of the nation and it assumed, of course, that the nation could never govern itself. Noticeably, it was always necessary for 'The Explorer' and the 'Young Men' to step in and provide leadership, example and government.

This being the case, the crucial issue was not the unity of the Empire, but how its *character was to be expressed*. One solution that was offered politically and practically in the 1890s was implicit in 'Our Lady of the Snows', published in *The Times* on 27 April 1897.[16] These verses had been written to celebrate the Canadian preferential tariff that had just been concluded and which was hoped by imperialists, like Kipling and Chamberlain, to be an augury of things to come at the Imperial Conferences held during the Jubilee celebrations. Obviously, the heady atmosphere of those weeks preceding the meetings, although he claimed immunity from it, touched Kipling sufficiently for him to lay aside some of the doubts that had been evident in 'The Song of the English'. The ideal that emerges in the poem is a mixture of sentiment and formal control and although the heaviest rhetorical emphasis falls on sentiment, it should not go unnoticed that it is the trade arrangement which calls forth both the parental and filial expression of feeling and that the title of the poem asserts possession by the metropolitan, Canada is 'Our Lady . . .'.

Certainly, it is true that according to this poem imperial unity was not to occur as a result of central control, of England either proposing or imposing some kind of political or constitutional arrangements. The verses stress, like Disraeli, Dilke and Froude had done before, that the essential character of the Empire was to be that of the family. It would be characterized by relationships, entered into willingly out of mutual respect, and with benefits for all concerned. Although 'A Nation spoke to a Nation', it was also a daughter speaking to her mother, proud to know that she still 'abide[s] by my mother's house' and that she has 'proven faith in the Heritage'.[17] Sentimental values would prove, the verses implied, the stimulus to economic arrangements.

Again Kipling was here reinforcing a line of argument that was receiving a great deal of emphasis at this time. Chamberlain, who like Kipling and Milner realized the necessity of 'educating' the electorate to the 'right' views on empire, had been heard to say on more than one occasion that 'I am willing to submit to the charge of being a sentimentalist when I say that I will never willingly admit of any policy that will tend to weaken the ties between the different branches of the Anglo-Saxon race which form the British Empire.'[18] Published in *The Times*, where so many of Chamberlain's speeches were also reported, the ideas must have reinforced one another and in doing so increased their audibility with the upper and upper middle classes of Victorian society who read this newspaper. The enthusiasm shown in the lines for the formalization of familial relationships in terms of trade regulations instructed a part of the nation in the way that the Empire might be best organized as it entered the twentieth century. The proffering of this advice just a few weeks before the Imperial Conference was another instance of Kipling trying to use his considerable power and reputation to generate an enthusiasm within the nation that went beyond complicity to specific proposals about what should become the character of the British Empire.

The heavier emphasis in this collection on the economic expression of the family character of the Empire derived from a cruder and more doctrinaire stress on race, military preparedness and expansionism. The essential character of the Empire had become its Anglo-Saxon core. In 'Our Lady of the Snows', what bound mother and daughter together was that in their lands 'white men go their ways . . . under the White Man's law'.[19] While this might sound like the authentic strain of Whig/Liberal justification of empire, of English laws and principles of government becoming the instruments for the freedom of mankind, it was in fact nothing of the sort, Kipling's imperialism was based unambiguously upon racial not cultural bonds. It was they which set aside geographical limits: 'the Empire is Us – . . . the White Man. . . . That is to say races speaking the English tongue, with a high birth rate and a low murder rate, living quietly under Laws which are neither bought nor sold.'[20] To qualify as a White Man you had to be of English descent, like Dilke in *Greater Britain* (1868). Kipling saw the world in terms of 'dearer' and 'cheaper' races, so that in 'Et Dona Ferentes' we read of having 'seen the racial ruction rise', with the 'men of half creation damning half creation's eyes', and this 'pentecostal crew' in their 'tantrums' included:

French, Italian, Arab, Spaniard, Dutch and Greek,
  and Russ and Jew,
Celt and savage, buff and ochre, cream and yellow . . .[21]

It is not difficult to understand why Koebner and Schmidt concluded that 'Race was the one fundamental basis of imperialism.'[22] The bad manners of 'native' peoples assured the British of their own superiority and gave them the justifiable right of anger at the barbarism of other races; as well as admitting the necessity to rule them or be more powerful than them. It was as a reaction to lines like these that the freethinker John McKinnon Robertson identified Kipling as a 'Barbarian Sentimentalist', adding that 'Race hatred seems to turn ostensibly civilized men into irrational barbarians.'[23] The heavy emphasis laid upon race, upon the essential character of the Empire residing in its Anglo-Saxon constituents, was reflected in the title that Kipling chose for the collection. Although, like Curzon, he continued to believe that 'Without India the Empire could not exist', by this time he also acknowledged, unequivocally, that the core of the Empire was the white Anglo-Saxon races: *The Five Nations*, Canada, New Zealand, Australia, Great Britain and America.[24] Even after the Venezuelan crisis Kipling, like Joseph Chamberlain, and like Dilke before both of them, refused 'to speak or to think of the United States as a foreign nation'.[25] Indeed, it became Kipling's hope in 1898–99 that expansionist imperialism would soon become an accepted part of US policy abroad. In this year, the Spanish–American War led to the USA establishing rights in Cuba and the Philippines. 'The White Man's Burden', finished in late November 1898, was sent first to Theodore Roosevelt and by him to Henry Cabot Lodge, it did not see the light of day in the press until 4–5 February 1899.[26] Kipling obviously thought in this instance it was important to confirm political conviction at the highest level as well as – and before – making his public declaration. He succeeded with Roosevelt who regarded the poem as 'good sense from the expansionist viewpoint', but the response of the US public was to reject imperialist adventures as alien to their political traditions.[27]

'The White Man's Burden' drew the line ever more distinctly between two types of empire and the relationship of one to another. There could have been no clearer statement of this than the first stanza of the poem:

Take up the White Man's burden –
  Send forth the best ye breed –
Go bind your sons to exile
  To serve your captives' need;
To wait in heavy harness,
  On fluttered folk and wild –

> Your new caught, sullen peoples,
> Half-devil and half-child.[28]

A month earlier on 18 January, *The Times* had already sounded the same note as these lines when it declared that '. . . the Empire . . . is now a mainstay of civilization and progress, the refuge of freedom, intellectual, political and commercial, in every part of the globe'.[29] On 11 February, the *Spectator* quoted Kipling's verses with approval, commenting that 'The duty of the white man is to conquer and control, probably for a couple of centuries, all the dark people of the world, not for his own good, but for theirs.'[30] Liberal critics, however, were quick to note that the moral content of such verses with their blend of destiny and mission in fact disguised a crude expansionism. As G.P. Gooch observed: 'Patriotism, conventionally defined as love of country, now turns out rather obviously to stand for love of more country.'[31] Some years earlier, Frederick Harrison, the positivist, had noted a change in the kind of patriotism being expressed in Britain in the 1890s and foretold the end to which it would lead. Writing about 'The Evolution of Our Race' in 1894, he had said, 'The wages of sin is death; and the wages of national buccaneering is disaster in the end. . . . True patriotism involves a nation of real and practical local limits.'[32]

It has sometimes been asserted that Kipling showed this kind of recognition of 'local limits' through the respect he showed in his stories for other cultures: he acknowledges their integrity in terms of their own social and historical environment. Perhaps, however, it is more important to ask from what this respect derived. Such recognition always occurred within the context of established imperial power and was usually a preference for the separate development of races, because of the unalterable superiority of the whites over the coloured races. The cheaper races could only move '[Ah, slowly!] toward the light', while 'the White Man' who 'dare not stoop to less' after curbing 'Sloth and heathen Folly', would be 'proffered laurel'. The relationship of superiority and inferiority was in other words seen as a perpetual one and it was the responsibility of the White Man:

> To seek another's profit,
> And work another's gain.

In short, to bring to the dependent Empire, peace, order, justice and public works, understanding always that at no time should he 'call too loud on Freedom' because the 'sullen peoples' were always likely to 'Bring all your hope to nought'.[33] The cultural relativism, in particular of the Indian stories, derived ultimately from the notion that East and West could never meet because the former could never attain the civilization of the latter.

All dispensations to conquered peoples, therefore, were to be imposed upon them. In *The Five Nations*, there appeared to be two ways of achieving this end. In 'The Pharaoh & the Sergeant', the native could be trained through 'faith, hope, whacking and despair' by the non-commissioned officers, as befitted his lowly status, 'to stand upon his feet and play the game' and 'Maxim his oppressor as a Christian ought to do'.[34] The other way was for the English to 'terribly carpet the earth with the dead' and then 'before their canon cool . . . to call the living to school'.[35] This the poem admits was a form of madness peculiar to the English and it referred to a particular instance of it: Kitchener's attempt, after the conquest of the Sudan, to raise money in England for the building of a college on Western lines for the Sudanese. The poem also recognized that this appearance of magnanimity in victory, asking 'no price in return' for the benefits they bestowed on the land, was in fact the way the English achieved 'the magic whereby they work their magic – wherefrom their fortunes spring'.[36] Importantly, however, the dispensations of both sets of verses occurred only when the framework of coercion had been established, and they worked then because the natives understood the element of compulsion that was involved. The speaker in 'Kitchener's School' reminds those about to receive a Western education that the Sirdar, 'who did not slay you in sport, . . . will not teach you in jest', just as the speaker in 'The Pharaoh & the Sergeant', warns English readers that any attempt to 'make a man' of the native should not beguile them into thinking that 'her Empire still is the Strand and Holborn Hill'. It depends entirely on those who continue to 'drill the black man white'.[37]

The harsh Darwinian world in which nation preyed upon nation in *The Seven Seas* had emerged in 'The Song of the Cities', but had been kept in check by the confidence of the imperialist led by his 'Vision' and assured always of the 'Whisper' of the Almighty. In this collection, however, only a few notes of this higher song are heard. All as one reviewer commented had become a matter of vigilance and fear, 'the contest for survival expresses itself with new power. Civilization must contend with civilization that the more efficient, the more skilful, the more resourceful, may inherit the earth.'[38] The 'Merchantmen' are not to be seen, only those that protect them from destruction by others; the reader's attention is drawn to the guardians of safety, from 'The Bell-Buoy' who sings by 'the gates of doom' and rides 'On the horns of death' to the warships that lie beyond. The 'Cruisers' are a 'guard and a lure':

For this is our office: to spy and make room,
As hiding yet guiding the foe to their doom;
Surrounding, confounding, to bait and betray
And tempt them to battle the seas' width away.[39]

Deviousness set upon destruction is the order of the day. The voices we hear are excited by the prospect of 'The blindfold game of war', because for them it is a natural state in which their 'art', restrained by peace, can now be achieved. In these verses, as in the 'Hymn Before Action' and those called 'The Destroyers', the rhetoric is high-flown as in 'The white-hot wake' and 'the wildering speed The Choosers of the Slain!' are apostrophized.[40]

Kipling's first poetic statement on the declaration of war, called 'The Old Issue', was made as usual in *The Times* on 29 September 1899. Previous commentators have stressed the inaccessibility of his lines to a modern audience. However, the basic metaphor, reiterated in every verse, is a simple and powerful one gathering as it does around the notion of the freeborn Englishman, who, since the time of King John, has fought fiercely to defend his right of 'Leave to live by no man's leave, underneath the Law.' The poem turns, therefore, upon the historic love of the English for 'All we have of freedom, all we use or know', which 'our fathers bought for us long and long ago'. Kruger and the Boers are associated throughout with the 'Kings' in British history who had threatened 'Ancient Right'. The people, on the other hand, are cast as 'Stewards of the Judgment' who with 'Lance and torch and tumult' have 'Wrenched it [liberty], inch and ell and all, slowly from the King.' Their mission now is to 'Suffer not the old King here or overseas.' Britain's imperial duty at this moment of crisis was to extend and perpetuate its free institutions in South Africa by preventing a tyrant such as Kruger 'Laying on a new land evil of the old.' The verses thus provided a means of possessing the past in relation to the present, addressing the nation and encouraging it to take up its heroic place now in world history as it responded to 'Trumpets in the vanguard that have sworn no truce with Kings!'[41]

The inveighing of the poem against Kings implies no radicalism or strong defence of Parliament. The 'Kings' referred to are specific instances that constitute a 'breed' that tyrannizes: King John, King Charles 1 and now Kruger are the epitome of it. Their crime was a refusal to recognize 'How our King is one with us, first among his peers.' At no point in the poem is mention made of the institution that insisted on this parity – though this is hardly surprising given the author's contempt for it. Indeed, the role now expected of Britain was thoroughly romantic and aristocratic. Traditionally great within its own bounds, having bought for itself 'freedom – not at little cost', it was now its duty to exercise that greatness abroad striking those tyrants there who sought to 'rule above the Laws'.[42] The call, therefore, was to loyalty to the State rather than to any representative institution within it and was part of that collectivist appeal of imperialism that has been noted before. The demand made upon patriotism by the Empire was above class interest and was identifiably conservative. It preserved ancient rights – that included those of Lords as well as Commons – and the racial superiority that had won them was, now, by military power, to spread their benefits throughout the world. 'The Old Issue' provides ample evidence of Hugh Cunningham's observations about the way in which, after 1870, patriotism had shifted towards the right of the political spectrum.[43]

Thus, the political reality of the situation – the British Empire going to war against a small nation whose obstinacy provided no real *casus belli*; the determination, nevertheless, of Milner supported finally by Chamberlain, to find a reason to fight – all of these particularities had been submerged under the greater weight of those symbolic incidents from British history when 'the people' refused to 'Give . . . ear to bondsmen bidding us endure.' Kipling with his images of 'Long-forgotten bondage, dwarfing heart and brain', sought to conjure the kind of national unity that Churchill achieved with his patriotic rhetoric during the darkest days of the Second World War and which, more recently, Margaret Thatcher and George Bush have tried to mobilize.[44] His next poetic statement, 'The Absent-Minded Beggar', which raised £250,000 for soldiers' families, revealed his ability to play upon those emotions that are often to the fore when Britain declares war upon another nation.

The sentiments expressed in the verses gained maximum exposure on their first appearance because they were published in Harmsworth's *Daily Mail.* This newspaper, which had been established in 1896, sold at a halfpenny and had the largest circulation of the new mass dailies. Although Harmsworth was later to persuade himself that his press had always taken a neutral stand, it played a significant role in fanning that popular enthusiasm for empire which as Koebner and Schmidt (and more recently McKenzie) have shown, came to a climax in 1899.[45] By this time, events such as Omdurman and Fashoda had ensured that Africa was fully incorporated into the sphere of national and imperial policy. France and Germany were perceived by many to be not only hostile, but actively involved in hindering the development of the British Empire in Africa. Although in 1896 Harmsworth had declared the *Daily Mail* to be 'independent and imperial', although his declared goal was a fusion of imperial interests, nevertheless, his own and the paper's closeness to the Conservative Party was well-known.[46] At the time, the *Daily Mail* was seen by some commentators to be a diversionary agent that distracted working people with the imperial dimension:

> It is a curious thing, but a fact beyond dispute, that when the masses are on the verge of rising in their majesty and asking for their rights, the classes only have to throw into their eyes the powder of imperialism, and to raise the cry of the fatherland in danger.[47]

There is no difficulty in identifying these elements at work in 'The Absent-Minded Beggar'; but while this may come as no surprise, another aspect of its publication in the *Daily Mail* was not without irony. This newspaper was frequently berated for its simplistic, disjunctive prose and for the awful effects it was said to be having on the grammar, syntax and style of the English language and, according to contemporaries and later historians of the press, it had a particular attraction for 'the small clerks who think twice or thrice before spending a penny a day on newspapers'.[48] On 31 October 1899, therefore, just before the declaration of war, its first readers were just those people who Richard Price has indicated were the real jingo crowds and the very kind of people from whom Kipling had sought to disassociate himself in 'Recessional'.[49] The type who were 'drunk with the sight of power' and who indulged in 'the frantic boast and foolish word'. The derogatory comments that Kipling made later about 'The Absent-Minded Beggar' and his refusal to include it in *The Five Nations*, seemed to indicate his awareness of these dimensions. He wryly observed that were it not suicide he would have shot the man who wrote it and in *Something of Myself* he concluded that, although the verses 'had some elements of direct appeal' they 'lacked poetry'.[50] Hardly surprisingly, reviewers at the time were in agreement with the author: one noted that he had become 'the jester-jongleur of the hour' and had confirmed the worst fears that many had always had of him.[51]

Such authorial reservations and critical disapproval were irrelevant, however, alongside the massive popular appeal of these verses and they should not obscure those qualities that allowed them to cross divides within the social formation of 1899. They are, perhaps, the supreme example of what T.S. Eliot described as Kipling's facility for using poetry as an 'instrument . . . which is intended to *act* to elicit the same response from all readers, and only the response which they can make in common'.[52] The contagion of the verses spread when 'Sir Arthur Sullivan wedded the words to a tune guaranteed to pull teeth out of barrel organs',[53] and the poem subsequently appeared in a variety of versions:

> . . . on tobacco jars, ash trays, packages of cigarettes, pillow-cases, plates and many other forms. One of these was a triptych, with a famous Woodville illustration of a British "Tommy", which was distributed as a souvenir by Lily Langtry at the hundredth performance of a play. . . . Lady Tree recited it in the Pakace Theatre for fourteen weeks and raised £70,000 . . . it went the round of barrel organs, music-halls, smoking concerts, drawing-room recitals.[54]

Published at a moment when war was about to be declared, and just after Chamberlain and Milner had spent months diligently nurturing public opinion about South Africa, 'The Absent-Minded Beggar' coincided splendidly with its historical moment, and, as has been indicated, raised more than a quarter of a million pounds in a few months.

In these verses, Kipling had returned to those techniques he had described in 'My Great & Only' and which had been particularly in his mind when he wrote the first set of *Barrack-Room Ballads.*[55] In 'The Absent-Minded Beggar' those 'basic and basaltic truths', driven home by a refrain, appeared in an undisguised form, quite blatantly attempting to bring into existence a national constituency of readers who would 'pay – pay – pay!' These readers were hectored throughout in a most single-minded and unrelenting way in order to convince them of their duty to *show* their support for the soldiers – 'Each of 'em doing his country's work'. To defer from such support was, it was implied, disloyal – not only to the soldiers but to the national cause at stake in this imperial war. The poem made a point of equating the two. The intra-class unity that was claimed to exist already in the Army, because it had brought together 'Cook's son – Duke's son – son of a belted Earl', was here presented as an ideal to which civilians ought to aspire. The appeal to them was made through a definition of patriotism that gathered to it the language and ideology of work, commerce and the family: the poem set out to define 'the job before us all', its refrain was built upon the notion of credit and expenditure and the money was to 'help the homes that Tommy left behind him.' All of these were concerns that transcended specific social groupings. Patriotism, whose expression was found in 'killing Kruger with your mouth', was rejected as a form of cowardice. Civilians, like soldiers, had to prove themselves on 'active service' and 'Pass the hat for [their] credit's sake'.[56]

'The Absent-Minded Beggar' set out quite deliberately to trade on, confirm and extend those feelings of community and cohesion that appear at moments of national crisis. Like most statements which receive popular acclaim at such a time, it included notions of being threatened by, as well as being aggressive towards, enemies, and, in this situation, civilians were given the role of defending the domestic realm. No longer was there any implied criticism of the state – that it had failed to cater for the needs of its military. Raising these funds was the civilians' duty, it was the way in which they were to show their loyalty to the war effort – their contribution to the cause. Obviously, the ethnocentric terms in which the poem sought to heighten national awareness was very powerful at such a time. However, although the appeal of the verses to unpaid rents, starving children and forsaken wives was a simple and emotive one, it was not simplistic.

Richard Price has noted that working-class nationalist expression was highly volatile, rooted in what Hoggart has called 'a moment by moment approach to life 'that involved no preconceived view of events and no unchanging frame of reference.'[57] A poem that set out to raise money, therefore, was most likely to attain its objective with the lower classes by making an appeal through those things, like 'gas and coal and vittles, and the house-rent falling due', that remained crucial and necessary, however much the concerns of the moment might change. Neither was the poem so simple as to allow middle- and upper-class audiences to escape by thinking that the responsibilities spoken of were not their own. 'Tommy' was being sent out to 'save the Empire', he was 'wiping something off a slate', correcting the mistakes of others.[58] In other words, the poem also called on more systematized ideological systems that were aware of a political reality behind this historic moment. The low critical esteem in which the poem has always been held, even by the author himself, should not now disguise the complexity and sophistication of this seemingly simplistic popular success.

The immediate fund-raising success of the poem must have derived also from the ubiquity of soldiers in Britain in the early days of the war as regiments prepared for embarkation. Once more the *Daily Mail* noted the enthusiasm in the country for these preparations:

> . . . even total strangers, carried away by the enthusiasm broke into the ranks and insisted on carrying rifle, kit bags . . . and at Waterloo all semblance of military order had disappeared. The police were swept aside and men were borne, in many cases, shoulder high to the entraining platform, while others struggled through in single file.[59]

By 7 October 1899, only 1.63 per cent of the Reserve had failed to answer the order for general mobilization. Moreover, there was a significant difference about the Army that was being mustered for this war. Men from different social strata flocked to the colours. The Militia, drawn principally from unskilled labour, the Volunteers, supported from skilled groups and the lower middle classes, and the Yeomanry, almost exclusively rural middle class and aristocratic, all sent contingents to join the Regular Army. By the time the war ended, these organizations had contributed 160,000 of the 400,000 troops that were serving in South Africa and 14 per cent of the British male population was in uniform.[60] The Army that Kipling observed in the Boer War was, therefore, significantly different in composition and behaviour from the one that had been his previous subject. Recruited from a variety of social groups, most of which had been touched by the Education Act, this was a more self-conscious soldiery, which had less need of a champion to voice its grievances and experiences. Something of these changes were registered in the altered heading under which the soldier verses were included in the volume and the sub-titles attached to each poem. No longer *Barrack-Room Ballads* they became instead *Service Songs* and the origin of the voice behind each set of verses was clearly noted. They are spoken by reservists, irregulars, yeomanry, married men, Australians and even members of the New South Wales contingent.

The regular serving soldiers of the verses identified the inclusion of these men in their ranks as one of the few salutary effects of the war. In 'The Parting of the Columns', the regular soldier admits that the newer elements 'shook us up to rights'.[61] The introductory lines with which the *Service Songs* began, however, reflected upon the wider implication of the recomposition of the Army. They pointed to a watershed in imperial terms; from now on this larger, more heterogeneous military force would be *necessary* to police the Empire:

> From 'Alifax to 'Industan,
> From York to Singapore –
> 'Orse, foot an' guns, The Service Man
> 'Enceforward, evermore![62]

No doubt this conclusion arose from the experiences of the Army in this war which differed greatly from the skirmishes on the North-West Frontier and the campaigns against 'Fuzzy-Wuzzy' on which the *Barrack-Room Ballads* had reported. The conflict in South Africa had shown that victory was no longer guaranteed in an imperial war and that such wars far from home were likely to demand, as this one had done, the resources of the whole nation. As in 1914, so in 1899, there was huge popular confidence about victory in the war. It was all to be over by Christmas. *Barrack-Room Ballads* had of course harped on the need for changes in military life. Nevertheless, since 1868, there had been in train a whole range of reforms which it had been hoped would improve the performance of the British Army. Thus, as one military historian has put it, 'it makes little sense to call the British Army in 1899 unreformed'.[63] The catastrophic series of reverses, therefore, that the

Army received in South Africa, was all the more alarming. It became clear that the military lacked the infrastructure to cope with sending large forces long distances for far campaigns. The British Army had no General Staff at this time and it found itself abroad with no adequate maps of the terrain on which it was to fight. These and many more adverse circumstances that sounder practice could have remedied produced a series of defeats unparalleled in Victorian campaigning, 'which made the blood run cold in the veins of every patriotic Englishman'.[64] The early British disasters in 'Black Week' were produced by unwise and even reckless choice of positions, scanty defensive preparations and over-reliance on the stolid bravery of the British Infantry. The losses told the story. At Talana, 145 Boer dead, 500 British, at Belmont the Grenadier Guards were badly knocked about by being caught in their own cross-fire, at Magersfontein, because of the lack of communication between parts of the brigade, those on the heights showered those below with shrapnel. Most alarming was the nature of these defeats: the Boers were greatly outnumbered and won. 'M.I.' (Mounted Infantry of the Line) recorded not only the way the British Army had to adapt itself hurriedly by forming new regiments to combat Boer guerillas, it lingered also on the disasters and losses that had produced these changes:

> Our Sergeant-Major's a subaltern, our Captain's a Fusilier –
> Out Adjutant's late of Somebody's 'Orse an' a Melbourne
> auctioneer.
>
> I used to belong in an Army once
> [Gawd! what a rum little Army once],
> Red little, dead little Army once!
> But now I am M.I.![65]

Public excitement and bitterness at home about these defeats was intense and Sir Redvers Buller was replaced as commander by Lord Roberts. He was not the last officer in this war to be removed from his post; indeed, the term 'Stellenbosched' was adopted as a euphemistic way of intimating that

> . . . whenever an officer was prominently connected with a losing battle, or exhibited marked incompetence in any field of military work, he got a billet at Stellenbosch, a bowery village deep down in Cape Colony, where was established our base supplies. The name therefore attained a deep significance and common usage in the army.

During the week that Kipling helped in the writing and production of *The Friend*, a newspaper for the British troops edited by war correspondents serving with Lord Roberts's forces, an item was included that contained a lighthearted explanation of the meaning of the term.[66] When, however, Kipling came to express the contemporary as already history in his poem called 'Stellenbosch', it was bitter irony rather than humour that was to the fore. Spoken by '*[Composite Columns]*', new fighting forces made up from the remnants of those previously destroyed in action, all that was apparent to these soldiers was:

> 'Ow we're sugared about by the old men
> ['Eavy-sterned amateur old men!]
> That 'amper an' 'inder an' scold men
> For fear of Stellenbosch!

These speakers saw quite clearly that their comrades had often been slaughtered by the shortsightedness and incompetence of their officers:

> The General 'ad "produced a great effect,"
> The General 'ad the country cleared – almost;
> The General " 'ad no reason to expect,"
> And the Boers 'ad us bloomin' well on toast!
> For we might 'ave crossed the drift before the twilight,
> Instead o' sitting down an' takin' root;
> But we was not allowed, so the Boojers scooped the crowd
> To the last survivin' bandolier an' boot.

However, these men who had survived levelled a much graver charge at their leaders, for they ascribed many of these defeats to a determination on the part of their officers to serve their own interests above all, even if this involved cowardice:

> The General saw the mountain range ahead,
> With their 'elios showin' saucy on the 'eight.
> So 'e 'eld us to the level ground instead,
> An' telegraphed the Boojers wouldn't fight.
> For 'e might 'ave gone and sprayed 'em with a pompom,
> Or 'e might 'ave slung a squadron out to see –
> But 'e wasn't takin' chances in them 'igh and 'ostile kranzes –
> He was markin' time to earn a K.C.B.[67]

A reader cannot but be reminded of Sassoon's 'General' some 14 years later, who, having done for his men with his 'plan of attack' then 'toddled' home safely to bed.[68] An example perhaps of literary influence or the continued incompetence of the high command in the British Army. Or maybe both. If to campaigns poorly led is added the decimation of the forces by diseases that might have been prevented by more basic hygiene in the camps, then it is not surprising to discover that many of the soldiers who served in the war, quite apart from those to be found in 'The Service Songs', registered a profound disillusion with what had occurred:

> A hard-headed view of the war, often coloured by bitterness and cynicism, emerges from the letters written by ordinary troopers. A sense of injustice and resentment at shabby treatment is a notable recurring theme in working-class writing, the feeling that, as one trooper phrased it "Tommy was anything but treated fair . . . they put us down to the lowest of the low".[69]

Such disillusionment marks the beginning and the end of the series of the *Service Songs*; and these, read alongside 'The Wage-Slaves', which had appeared in the first part of the collection, present a convergence of voices in various stages of disenchantment with British traditional institutions and practices. Although 'Chant-Pagan' and 'The Return' glorify their South African experiences as the 'makin' of a bloomin' soul', the glorification acts as a critique of England:

> 'Ow can I ever take on
> With awful old England again,
> An' houses both sides of the street,
> And 'edges two sides of the lane,
> And the parson an' "gentry" between,
> An touchin' my 'at when we meet –
> Me that 'ave been what I've been?

The final line here is a refrain in the early part of the poem and throughout the stanzas end with 'Me!', stressing the access of self-consciousness that has been produced in the English Irregular by his experiences in South Africa. This in its turn produces the awareness:

> That the sunshine of England is pale,
> And the breezes of England are stale,
> An' there's somethin' gone small with the lot;

Finally, it results in a rejection of the metropolitan in favour 'a Dutchman I've fought 'oo might give / me a job' – surely, a certain measure of this man's disenchantment with the heart of empire.[70]

'The Return', sub-headed as the sentiments of *All Arms*, also stresses the new awareness of those who have come back to England, for they are 'not the same'. They not only know 'The size . . . of the game', but also its 'meanin' '. Their experience of an imperial war and all it has taught them about such things as order, discipline, the importance of comradeship and the brutal reality of death, has made them dissatisfied with the land to which they return:

. . . now discharged, I fall away
To do with little things again . . .
Gawd, 'oo knows all I cannot say,
Look after me in Thamesfontein!

Both London and, earlier in the poem, ' 'Ackneystadt', are given names that associate them with some of the battles of the Boer War, suggesting, therefore, that the men who have already fought will encounter enemies just as fierce in their homeland. The ambivalence of the returning soldiers' response is underlined by the lines which appear after the first stanza and then again at the very end of the poem:

If England was what England seems,
An' not the England of our dreams,
But only putty, brass, an' paint,
'Ow quick we'd drop her! But she ain't![71]

The deliberate ellipsis of the lines determines that the affirmation of the final words can only be maintained by pretending that the *real* England is the England of dreams. As such, of course, it has yet to be made and while this hope of *All Arms* might be seen as no more than the typical desire of returning soldiers for a land fit for heroes, it is a response that, at the time, must have preyed upon the fears the middle and upper classes had about those lower down the social scale. The fear that having understood, as these voices did, the 'meanin' of the game', they might still rise 'in their majesty . . . asking for their rights'.[72] In this sense, the Boer War, which had appeared as a factor that could distract working men from a concern with social questions, was now seen to be a deferral that, once ended, could become the cause of those questions being asked with renewed vigour.

The meaning that the author attached to 'the game', however, had little to do with a socialist analysis of the problems facing working people. In 'The Wage Slaves', written within months of these two *Service Songs*, and included in the first part of the collection, so that it was less likely to be unseen by those who looked askance on his dialect verses, was a vitriolic attack on those who occupied places 'by . . . grace'. The essential division of the world was between those who worked and those who did not but were dependent upon the efforts of others. The line was drawn between 'the bondslaves' and 'the wage-slaves . . . who merely do the work / For which they draw the wage' and those who dwelt on:

. . . the guarded heights
Where guardian souls abide –
Self-exiled from our gross delights –

Above, beyond, outside:
An ampler arc their spirit swings –
Commands a juster view –
We have their word for all these things,
Nor doubt their words are true.[73]

Kipling's targets here were those like the then present leadership of the Conservative Party, such as the newly retired Prime Minister, Lord Salisbury, and his nephew, Arthur Balfour, who had recently assumed his mantle. The latter, who had been in his time an Oxford philosopher and was the author of a book on philosophical doubt, was well-known for his languid approach to national and international politics. Kipling associated both his manner and his background with the naivete of 'scholarly plough[ing] the sands'.[74] These men of inherited wealth and status were the but of further savage attacks in 'The Dykes' and 'The Old Men', written also in 1902 and dispersed throughout this collection.[75] The effect of such a dispersal was to keep them and their follies constantly in the reader's mind; not an enjoyable experience for those who felt that they were the subjects of these verses. The greatest of their follies, according to these verses, was a refusal to acknowledge that the world ever changed, that 'old stars fade or alien planets arise'. Such aristocratic groups lived in the past, they were an anachronistic burden on the country:

We shall peck out and discuss and dissect, and
evert and extrude to our mind,
The flaccid tissues of long-dead issues offensive to
God and mankind.[76]

Blind to the dangers that actually threatened their own world, that now might be 'plundered while [they] slept', their greatest sin was to have proved false to the heritage their fathers left them. The heritage was, of course, the Empire, and they had allowed 'The Dykes' which kept at bay enemies to be breached. In doing so, they had in the recent war 'slain our sons as our fathers we have betrayed'.[77] To a social group that prided itself on its sense of honour, the accusation of treason was certainly an arrow that might stick. It was an attempt to reawaken it to what the writer saw as its real purpose – the holding of sound views about the Empire.

Increasingly, Kipling and men like Lord Milner and Lord Roberts came to see those with inherited wealth and a privileged educational background as the ruin of the country: 'Because of your witless learning and your beasts of warren and chase', they had 'set . . . their leisure and . . . their lusts' above the nation's need.[78] Hedged around by privilege, they deliberately cut themselves off from the life of 'the loitering street'; but worst of all, because of the British respect for tradition, their claim to 'a juster view' went unchallenged. The 'bondslaves', among whom Kipling classed himself, were pledged to their responsibilities and they saw themselves as the victims of those whose words were never doubted, but, who were through their idleness and inefficiency, giving away an Empire. Bondslaves and wage-slaves endured 'From age to cheated age' as the 'Co-heirs of insolence, delay, / And leagued unfaithfulness'. The nation was, therefore, reconstituted in these satires to comprise those who worked and those, who because of hereditary privilege, found no need to do so.

All of these poems, however, were rather more than satiric, they were apocalyptic and visionary. The undoubting acceptance of the 'guardian souls' in the first verse of 'The Wage-Slaves' was broken in the fifth by 'the vast Event' that entered through 'the Gates of Stress and Strain'.[79] 'The Dykes', as in the poem of that name, were well and truly breached, but so also was the fabric of English political leadership. As a consequence of the 'jolly good lesson' served out to the British via the Boer War, 'The Wage-Slaves' foresaw that 'all old idle things' would be supplanted by those who hold 'Power . . . by right, not grace' and victory would go to the:

> Men like Gods that do the work
> For which they draw the wage –
> Begin – continue – close the work
> For which they draw the wage!

By implication, constitutions and hereditary rights disappeared, giving way to those who ruled because they were competent and were willing to sacrifice themselves to their chosen cause; 'such as dower each mortgaged hour / Alike with clean courage'. The degeneracy of the ruling political groups and the need to be rid of the institutions that supported their power were to become themes of growing importance in Kipling's political writing up to and during the First World War. Significantly, however, 'The Wage-Slaves' foresaw no more than the replacement of one elite by another, because the 'Power' to which the bondslave acceded was also a right to:

> . . . rule his heritage –
> The men who simply do the work
> For which they draw the wage.

Therefore, despite the populist appeal of the recognition of the bondslaves that 'Such is our need' that 'we . . . must seek indeed' to 'engage' the masses, the role and place of the people remained subordinate.[80]

The apocalypse longed for here had no democratic implications. In this sense, the use of the many voices in the *Service Songs* from all branches of the Army was there to strengthen and enlarge the chorus of dissatisfaction that had arisen from the prosecution of the Boer War. The critique, however, was directed not only at the political leaders of the day. It was more fundamental than that, because it saw British institutions and social organization as the engines that were destroying the British Empire. This was at its clearest in 'The Islanders', the satire that was infamous in its own time and whose vitriol still boils and bubbles to this day.

Angus Wilson summarizes brilliantly one aspect of the poem which makes it the culmination of those just discussed when he says of 'The Islanders' that it 'takes each sacred cow of the clubs and senior common rooms and slaughters it messily before its worshippers' eyes'.[81] Furthermore, Carrington made an equally important point when he noted that 'no earlier pronoucement of Rudyard's had touched so many victims on the raw'.[82] The poem played a not insignificant role in damaging his reputation with some members of his public whose adulation he had previously received. The most interesting thing about these verses, however, in terms of a developing imperial philosophy, is the course plotted for the nation as it seeks to replace 'the flannelled fools at the wicket' and 'the muddied oafs at the goal'. What is needed is 'each man born in the Island broke to the matter of war'. The only way now to maintain the Empire and keep at bay the threat of invasion is to create a society that is in essence militaristic. Neither aristocracy, religion, parliamentary or socialist process can offer anything useful:

> Will ye pray them or preach them, or print them,
> or ballot them back from your shore?
> Will your workmen issue a mandate to bid them
> strike no more?
> Will ye rise and dethrone your rulers? [Because ye
> were idle both?]

The answer was to learn 'Warcraft' to send sons to the Army's service, offer 'fields for their camping-place', what Britain needed was 'men who could ride and shoot',

> So at the threat ye shall summon – so at the need
> ye shall send
> Men, not children or servants, tempered and taught to
> to the end;

The only way to wipe out the memory of recent defeats, combat the threats from European powers and make sure that the land was no longer 'fenceless' was to introduce conscription and to deny the privilege of those who out of idleness 'grudge[d] a year of service to the lordliest life on earth'.[83] This theme was to be taken up again in far more detail in the story 'The Army of a Dream' and actively pursued in the support Kipling gave Lord Roberts for his conscription campaign.

In essence, therefore, the verse in the *Five Nations* was yet another attempt to transform the character of the Empire and the metropolitan under the growing apprehension that they were internationally besieged. As the situation in Africa worsened, the tone of the verse had become more strident; it was more aggressively racist and more obviously brutal in its attitudes towards newly acquired territories and people. The Boer War fulfilled the worst imaginings of all previous volumes and the solutions proposed for the problems that had been revealed seemed to some alien to, and disruptive of, the traditional social and political order of Great Britain. The *Service Songs* of the *Five Nations* showed a returning soldiery, drawn from different classes and social levels, that claimed – and it could have seemed threatening to some – to know the 'meanin' of the game'.[84] Explicitly ranging itself alongside them was an equally disillusioned group, with whom the author was closely associated, which entirely rejected the present political and class leadership and the institutions from which it derived its power. What must have been most alarming to some was the consonance of interest claimed between these two groups as against existing social formations. These verses stressed that working men who had fought recognized the value that 'Warcraft' had had for them: duty, order, discipline had been the 'makin' of their bloomin' souls' and there were verses in the *Five Nations* that suggested that if they were led by 'Men like Gods who do the work', then the Empire could be saved and the nation become 'mighty by sacrifice'.[85]

It was, however, quite obvious that the essential prerequisite to this occurrence was the total organization of British society on militaristic lines. The culture of the upper-class gentleman who played the game by the rules was rejected in favour of training for war which began early on:

> Each man born in the Island entered at youth to the game
> not to be mastered in haste,
> But after trial and labour, by temperance, living chaste.

This was the only way to 'bide sure-guarded when the restless lightnings wake'.[86] G.K. Chesterton was just one of those who saw that this 'worship of militarism' was a denial of what many people thought of as an English way of life. It led him to the conclusion that there was a 'great gap in his [Kipling's] mind and what may roughly be called the lack of patriotism'. Clearly, the new world order proposed in the *Five Nations* was seen by Chesterton, and those like him, to involve a notion of national identity and an international role with which they did not wish to be associated. Kipling was 'the philanderer of nations' whose interest was with the power England could wield throughout the world, he only 'admires England because she is strong not because she is English'. All that was unique and traditional would give way to the collectivist principles that were essential to 'the idea of discipline'.[87]

Well before Chesterton responded in this way to the collection there were, not surprisingly, other objections from the organs which represented those who had seen their sacred cows so messily slaughtered. Along with Chamberlain, Milner and Kitchener, Kipling was detested by the pro-Boers and those who had re-evaluated their notions of empire, or who were developing new attitudes in response to recent events. They had been quick to note the antagonism in his verse 'to the spirit of democracy' and they contemptuously dismissed his 'horrible . . . jingo-jingles'. If they failed, as Price has shown, to convert the working classes with their rhetoric during the Boer War, there were literary critics who were as appalled as they were by the stridency of Kipling's output.[88] The Armed Forces certainly sang 'Recessional', Dowden commented, no doubt with some truth the Kipling verses had 'served to evoke or guide the feelings of nations, and to determine action in great affairs', but this was by no means the whole picture.[89] *Punch's* response to 'The Islanders', for all its humour, registered the offence caused by the poem and suggested that the 'Poet of the British Race' had overstepped the mark.

Over and over again he had in the last few years told the British that they were a 'wretched, imbecilic, played-out set of nincompoops', but on this occasion he had exceeded his licence. The press and some of the reviewers had 'ladled out sloppy praise to KIPLING until he's ready to burst' and the result had been that he had 'got a bit above himself'.[90] By 1903, therefore, when the *Five Nations* was published, one reviewer confidently wrote that:

> And now the POPULIS AURA is veering. Mr Kipling is no longer the latest favourite; indeed, it is rather doubtful if, in the hearts as against the heads of the people, there are not certain classes with whom he has actually ceased to be a conspicuous favourite at all.[91]

With Liberals of the old school and the pro-Boers he never had been a favourite, the response of those lower down the social scale who read his verse in the newspaper or sang it to catchy tunes in the music hall is unknown to us, so that this alteration in his reputation must have been caused by the recession of some of the hereditary ruling class whom he had made the targets of verses like 'The Islanders', 'The Dykes', 'The Old Men' and 'The Wage-Slaves'. This change was used by the reviewer as an opportunity to make it clear once and for all that Kipling did not belong in the literary establishment. Thus Arthur Waugh declared in the *Book Monthly* that:

> It would be an affectation to pretend that the time has not arrived when people are beginning to hold their own attraction for his poetry at arm's length and to ask themselves whether, after all, he is exactly what we understand by a poet as contrasted with a rhetorician or song writer? . . . The question begins to be discussed at dinner tables all over the country: Is he a poet at all?[92]

The posing of this question immediately connected this review with existing critical discourse about Kipling's poetry and was the means of presenting him as no more than the inevitable product of a cheap newspaper press. It was likely that massive reputations would be made for a day and collapse as quickly once the literary franchise had been extended to people without education and without the experience of truly great writers. The promotion of writers by the newspapers like that which had published 'The Absent-Minded Beggar' had produced:

> . . . an entirely new body of readers. . . . With the spread of lower-middle-class ambition this . . . is inevitable, but it is against this very energy that literature should make its stand. It is the province of literature, particularly poetry . . . to preserve the balance and power of the national character.[93]

Such a line of argument that presented Kipling as no more than the darling of the lower middle class studiously ignored the fact that the occasion for this particular critical reflection was the failure of his reputation with the upper rather than the lower reaches of Edwardian society. It was fundamentally an extension and re-invigoration of the argument used by Buchanan and those before him who had stressed that once the 'Mean Whites' were addressed literary definitions began to alter as they became assimilated.[94] The change that had been detected in Kipling's popularity was another opportunity to claim that reviewers had been correct all along. His verse was no more than the typical ephemera produced by popular culture:

> No matter how popular or effective his dialect may be at present it will not be so when present conditions pass. . . . From Homer to Tennyson the greatest poets have invariably been masters of sim-

ple, correct and refined speech, which they made into literature of universal appeal.[95]

The vacillations of literary taste which had so discomforted the critics when they were in Kipling's favour were now recognized as the true indicators of his worth, or lack of it, and he could safely be classified as a failure. 'He might have sustained the cause not only of literature but also of national dignity', because his 'preference for patois and the forms of illiteracy' meant that he had only been able to achieve the status of a 'minor poet'. His flirtation with 'Demos', with 'banjo and the kettle-drum vivacity' had turned him into 'a menace to literature'.[96]

The decline in the popularity of Kipling's verse with the upper levels of society was therefore used as an occasion to show that real literature must remain as it always had been, unsullied by popular forms. There was some confidence in this review that 'the bad literary manners' of 'the Prophet of the Inarticulate' were discredited and that 'simple, correct and refined speech . . . of universal appeal' was back in place.[97] The offence given by some of the verses to the Tory upper classes was taken as a heaven-sent opportunity by critics, frequently with different political affiliations, to try to drive the former champion from the literary field once and for all. The publication of the *Five Nations* was a watershed in Kipling's career as a poet; with it he had explicitly antagonized both major political groupings and allied himself with those who became known as the Radical Right, who were regarded in the years before 1914 with the deepest suspicion by much of the Establishment and Press.

FIVE

'The Endless Night Begins'

The Years Between 1919

Sixteen years passed before Kipling published what was to be his last collection of new verse, and, in that time, the questioning as to whether he was *really a poet* had become a refusal by the literary establishment to acknowledge the existence either of the poetry or its author. Denigration had been transformed into a total refusal to grant it critical attention. Reviewing *The Years Between* in *The Athenaeum*, T.S. Eliot commented that 'Mr Kipling . . . is a neglected celebrity':

> The arrival of a new book of his verse is not likely to stir the slightest ripple on the surface of our conversational intelligentsia. He has not been crowned by the elder generation; malevolent fate has not even allowed him to be one of the four or five or six greatest living poets . . . he is merely not discussed. Mr Kipling has not been analysed.[1]

The new collection contained 45 poems excluding the 'Epitaphs', and all but the latter had appeared previously in newspapers and periodicals, sometimes simultaneously in different ones here in Britain and the USA. The critical silence with which *The Years Between* was met sharply illustrates how the literary was defined by the exclusion of the popular: the combination of widespread consumption with widespread critical disapproval or dismissal was then, as now, a fairly certain sign that a cultural commodity was popular.

T.S. Eliot suggested at one point in the review that one of the chief reasons for the rejection of Kipling's verse was stylistic: it related to his refusal to adopt the lyric manner and accede to the music of Shelley and Campion. In short, as on previous occasions, he was accused of not conforming to what 'poetical coteries' defined as the dominant and acceptable mode of English poetry.[2] The subjectivism of Kipling's verse, Eliot argued, differed from most native varieties: it was personal in the way an orator's words were personal, 'not by revelation, but by throwing themselves in and gesturing the emotion of the moment'. Such writing had 'the sound-value of oratory, not of music'. His poems 'persuade not by reason, but by emphatic sound'. They have:

> . . . like the public speaker an idea to impose; and they impose it in the public speaker's way, by turning the idea into sound, and iterating the sound . . . their business is not to express, but to lay before you, to *state*, . . . to propel, to impose on you an idea.[3]

The dislike Kipling's verse aroused was connected, therefore, with his appropriation of poetry to a different use. Underlying the question that critics had always asked – Is he *really* a poet? – was a perceived threat to dominant forms and the expectations readers had of them. The variations and differences in Kipling's style frequently challenged the basis of contemporary definitions of the poetic and, of course, their liberal inflections: English poetry defined its ground in terms of its openness to different ideas. Yet, ironically, the only way it was able to maintain such pluralism was by the active exclusion of anything which involved a single resolution. Kipling's verse collections always revealed the limits of that pluralism. The exclusiveness of the literary institution was something T.S. Eliot himself was to become increasingly aware of in the next 10 years or so but Kipling's verse, which was essentially occasional, resisted both the emerging orthodoxy of Modernism and that of Georgianism which dominated the pre-war years. The characteristics of Georgian poetry with which, significantly, many of the First World War poets who felt antipathetic to Kipling were associated, were quite the opposite to the verse of *The Years Between*. The Georgians were regional in their subject matter and celebrated England via 'The glory of the beauty of the morning, / The cuckoo crying over the untouched dew.'[4] The largest of their larger concerns was a mild interest in social reform. In the belatedly romantic preoccupation with nature, in the tendency to define England through its localities, through the sound of 'all the birds / Of Oxfordshire and Gloucestershire', there was an essentialism that was quite the opposite of the concern in Kipling's verse with international relations and world dominion.[5] The determinedly local response to the land and the national identity it implied can be seen as a manifestation of that revulsion against imperialism that occurred as a result of the Boer War. Indeed, what really underlay these contrasting poetic styles and the critical indifference that attended this volume of verse, was a fundamental ideological conflict that had always been at the root of Kipling's relations with a reviewing institution heavily imbued with the liberal notion of literature as an 'open pulpit'.[6] T.S. Eliot alluded to this when he said:

> A serious contemporary has remarked of the present volume that "in nearly all our poetical coteries the poetry of Kipling has long been anathema, with field sports, Imperialism and public schools".[7]

Kipling's verse was associated in literary minds with all those institutions that promoted collectivist ideals, and which, in doing so, challenged basic liberal precepts. In a decade that saw the accumulation of domestic crises, that by 1911 had tended to move from Parliament to the streets and barracks, verse that made 'a naive appeal to so large an audience' became increasingly suspect to liberal-minded critics and their readers.[8] Kipling, in both his verse and his life, supported those who showed a willingness to bypass existing political structures and *The Years Between* made no concession towards the lack of enthusiasm there now was for empire. In fact, it reasserted it as England's only hope of survival. The volume contained 'The Houses', a poem that dated back to 1898, which without qualification or apology asserted the economic and international political importance of the British Empire:

> 'Twixt my house and thy house the pathway is
>   broad
> In thy house or my house is half the world's hoard;
> By my house and thy house hangs all the world's
>   fate,
> On thy house and my house lies half the world's
>   hate.
>
> For my house and thy house no help shall we find
> Save thy house and my house – kin cleaving to
>   kind:
> If my house be taken, thine tumbleth anon,
> If thy house be forfeit, mine followeth soon.[9]

Such a poem, which still looked towards the kind of imperial federation of which Chamberlain had dreamed and which had been an issue in *The Seven Seas*, must have set the seal on Kipling's exclusion from the literary scene. After 1901, nobody advocated that the Empire should grow and with the defeat of any possibility of imperial preference its heterogeneity was a source of fear and anxiety. As Kipling himself had noted with great bitterness and venom, since their return to power in 1905 the Liberals had tried to shed 'The imperial gains of the age which their forefathers piled them.'[10] 'The Houses' was the manifesto of an unrepentant imperialist. It was included in the volume to show that renowned anti-imperialists like Hobson and Morley had been wrong. During the Great War, apart from Ireland, it had been possible to rely on the loyalty of the Empire and many thousands of troops from all parts of it had fought and died. The publication of such a poem in 1919 implied that when the chips had been down it was 'kin cleaving to kind' that had mattered.[11] It is noticeable, however, that the verses had been in no way amended to address the question that India was now to put: what reward for the sacrifice? In relation to its moment of production, therefore, the oracular verse in this volume was, as much popular writing often is, deeply contradictory: its stylistic 'aberrations' challenged dominant poetic forms and critical precepts, while its ideological tendencies were both anachronistic and aggressively reactionary.

Moreover, the contradictions in relation both to style and ideology do not end there. While T.S. Eliot was quite correct to point out that much of the verse in this and previous collections was oracular in its active propagandization of a quite particular point of view, nevertheless this was by no means a complete inventory of the type of work included in the collection. Two other forms of poetic writing were to be found in it. *The Years Between* was unique in containing the very kind of verse Kipling was supposed never to write – lyric poems. These were not many, but poems like 'A Nativity', 'My Son Jack', 'A Recantation' and 'Gethsemane' seem to have been personal in origin.[12] Inspired by the grief caused by the death of his son, John, in the Battle of Loos, the author must have deemed them to have such common currency that they could be justified as representative of the reaction that was occurring generally in many parts of the nation as it struggled to assimilate the massive losses on the multiple battlefronts of the First World War. All of these lyric poems end by apparently affirming the British war effort, but in each that final affirmation has been preceded by an absurdist vision, where all that is left is steadfastness and resignation in a world bereft of meaningful signs.

The other group of poems which were neither oracular nor lyric were the 'Epitaphs' whose classical form ensured their composure, simplicity and brevity. Once again, however, their form set them apart from the poetic response of soldier and civilian poets. To convey the enormity of the war, the reader of the 'Epitaphs' is confronted with brief lives, lost throughout the world rather than only on the Western Front, and the impression is of ultimate contradictions: a world and a humanity that is simultaneously ennobled *and* brutalized. Momentarily, those who 'Life shall cure, / Almost of Memory' are required to look at the tragedy of those who had no choice but to 'endure' the 'Immortality' that life thrust upon them.[13] It is a glimpse whose moral, metaphysical and historical implications interrogates the worth of this kind of immortality.

In terms, therefore, of literary history, the neglect of *The Years Between* confirmed the low opinion critics already held of Kipling's poetry and aided his invisibility as a poet to modern readers. However, the continuing willingness of the press, here and in the USA, to jump at the chance of publishing this author's latest verse utterances suggests that they were seen at the time to be relevant to the immediate social situation of the people and to express their felt collectivity.[14] While the stylistic variation of the verse seemed to threaten and resist the expectations of the 'conversational intelligentsia', the ideological contradictions of which this was so often a sign were able to generate and circulate meanings in the ongoing process of cultural exchange.[15] As Rider Haggard noted, the verse written during this period articulated 'in terse rhyme *exactly* what other men were thinking'.[16] It was, therefore, symptomatic of the shifting allegiances of the people during the crisis in the nation in the years between 1898 and 1918. If nothing else, the title of this collection was apt.

Although historians are not always agreed as to the importance that should be ascribed to the various crises that beset the Edwardian years, two of its characteristics do not seem to be in dispute: the anxiety with which many people faced the new century and the growing fear among some that the existing political and social structure was so antiquated that radical innovation was the only solution. Both the popular and the quality press depicted the future in terms of the decline and fall of a once great nation and empire. The *Westminster Review* commented that 'England has grown old, her national vitality is exhausted. She has arrived at the stage of senile decay . . .'; and the *Daily Mail* put it in an even more sententious way – 'at this very critical moment in some inscrutable manner the old fire and energy seems to be waning within us. We are entering stormy seas, and the time may be near when we shall have to fight in very truth for our life.'[17] It was, however, perhaps the Bishop of London who had been the most alarmist when he remarked that, 'The party system is breaking down. People are ceasing to be interested in the way in which the party game is played. . . . Yet we do not face the fact.'[18] A refusal to confront problems was not an accusation that could be levelled against the verse in *The Years Between*. Inspired by the same doubts as all these commentators, it nevertheless did not find the causes of the predicaments which faced the country as being 'inscrutable'.

The 'Dedication', added in 1919, reminded readers and rulers that the problems of 'the bitter years before' the war were caused, just as those of 'the over-sweetened hour' of victory were likely to be, by a trust in revelation from above, by a faith in leaders who asked people to believe that willing a thing to be so would be enough to make it prevail.[19] The warning was clearly related to the development of peace talks around Woodrow Wilson's 'Thirteen Points', which Kipling regarded as a highly dangerous evasion of the previous history of Europe and the likely future reality in that continent. However, whereas in previous collections the faith in the judgement of the people rather than their leaders had emerged in the soldier songs, these voices were not to be heard in this volume. What replaced them was a deliberate and repeated use of Biblical incident and reference.

Two effects were produced by this usage which led in quite different directions. On the one hand, it lent a note of prophecy to the verse, often a quite heavy-handed one; on the other, these verses frequently inverted both the intention and the traditional understanding of their Biblical paradigms and the social and political meaning that was often attached to them. The Dedication 'To the Seven Watchmen' with which the volume opened was the first example of this practice. It was based on the Book of Revelation in which seven angels, the representatives of God, instructed St John the Divine in what was to come to pass. The whole purpose of the Dedication, however, was to throw doubt on the capacity of those on high, particularly in this instance those in authority at Versailles, to offer any useful guidance to ordinary humanity. Indeed, the reliance of men on their own judgement was claimed as a far more secure source for action: 'a man's mind will tell him more / Than Seven Watchman sitting in a tower'.[20]

In its preference for and trust in the perceptions of the led rather than the leaders, these verses picked up a populist thread that had been there at least since the *Barrack-Room Ballads*. In effect, these lines invoked the people against those who supposedly had knowledge and power. The mantle of the satirist which had been used in 'The Dykes' and 'The Islanders' was cast aside and that of the Old Testament prophet was assumed to produce another diatribe against those whom wielded illegitimate authority through wealth and inherited position.

The same technique worked to sharper effect in 'The Sons of Martha'.[21] It made use of a better known instance from the Bible and treated its subject more extensively and less allegorically. The reference was to the short story told in St Luke (Ch. 10, v. 38–42) of Christ's visit to the house of two sisters. Mary welcomed Him and sat all day at His feet listening to His teaching, while Martha scurried about tending to the practical needs of the Master and his disciples. Worn out, she finally erupted, complaining that her sister had given her no help. Christ replied, however, that Mary had chosen 'the one thing [that] is needful', she 'hath chosen that good part, which shall not be taken away from her.'[22]

'The Sons of Martha', which was widely published first in *Associated Sunday Magazines*, then in the *Standard* and then separately, meditates on this distinction between the two sisters and insists that it has formed the basis of all social division ever since: there are those born to be served and those who serve, hence the title of the verses. However, the poem attacks the descendants of the virtuous Mary as parasites 'who toil not neither do they spin', and in so doing it casts doubt on both divine judgement and the justice of the social organization built upon it.[23] These lines were written in 1907, shortly after the Liberal landslide of the previous year and the results of this election are often taken as evidence that at last the character of the Commons was beginning to reflect changes in the electorate. In the election, the Conservatives lost 200 seats and this suggested the ending of the control of Parliament by the landed interest. Nearly half of those returned were new to the Commons; there was increasing strength from business, law and finance and the Labour Party became an independent force with the return of 29 members. These changes, however, were not noticed in the poem, which suggests that its subject was the larger social structure of which the political was the epiphenomenon. It bitterly prophesied the continuation in Britain of the existing order – the perpetuation of authority in the hands of those who had inherited it, power continuing to reside with the privileged rather than being determined by merit:

> . . . the Sons of Mary smile and are blessed – they
> know the angels are on their side.
> They know in them is the grace confessed, and for
> them are the Mercies multiplied.
> They sit at the Feet – they hear the World – they
> see how truly the Promise runs:
> They have cast their burden upon the Lord, and –
> the Lord He lays it on Martha's Sons![24]

This kind of poem, compared with those in *The Seven Seas*, does not target a specific political group. 'The Song of the English' had isolated the Liberals and clearly designated them as the cause of England's woes, which it confidently expected the newly fledged Conservative era to resolve. The revival of Liberal fortunes in 1906 did not at this point produce verses directed solely against them; rather like 'The Islanders' and 'The Dykes', this poem attacked the Establishment as a whole, Kipling had emerged from the Boer War believing in the toughness of ordinary people and the debilitation of the upper classes and these verses were a continuation of both of these convictions. Essentially, the poem attacked a system that allowed 'The Sons of Martha', 'in all ages to take the buffet and cushion the shock', while those with inherited authority were 'pleasantly sleeping and unaware'; and it questioned the judgement and justice of a god whose 'Pity allows them [i.e. the Sons of Mary] to leave their work when they damn-well choose', while their opposite numbers had to 'finger death at their gloves' end where they / piece and repiece the living wires'.[25]

In showing this clear preference for he who gave 'simple service simply given to his own kind in / their common need', the poem implied that religion was a system of belief that supported an insupportable social system and it unequivocally argued that virtue resided in the collective traditions of those whose 'care' it was 'to embark and entrain / Tally, transport, and deliver duly the Sons of Mary'.[26] Typical of a populist response, the lines cumulatively implied that the country was held to ransom by an elite that was unworthy of the privileges it had accrued to itself. In 1902, Kipling commented to a friend, 'What makes me sick is . . . the way, to wit, in which the responsible politician admits the cold truth of one's contention and then explicitly says that he doesn't dare "go in advance of public opinion" and so on.' By 1909, he was convinced that politicians in general were 'only united in one thing and that is lying'.[27]

Certainly, during these years, Kipling was not alone in arguing that despite the party divide, the House of Commons was in essence a club dominated by a social fraction whose differences were really very small. H. Belloc and G.K. Chesterton put this argument with great vehemence in their book *The Party System*. The situation was typified for many in a much photographed incident of H.H. Asquith and A.J. Balfour leaving the Palace of Westminster arm-in-arm after an evening of verbal swordplay.[28] Sir Willoughby de Broke, leader of the Diehard group in the Lords, commented acidly: 'They do love each other so.'[29] The feeling that there was not much to choose between the two front benches and the disillusion it produced with the party system, which the Bishop of London had noted at the turn of the century, produced in the Edwardian years a grouping which historians now describe as the Radical Right. The particular heroes of this group were Joseph Chamberlain and Alfred, Lord Milner, who frequently spoke of the 'rotten system of party politics'.[30]

This group had no formal organization, but were a collection of super patriots and included some of Kipling's friends and acquaintances, like Leo Maxse, owner and editor of the xenophobic *National Review*, as well as Lord Milner and Chamberlain. The foundation of their position was tariff reform allied with the strengthening of the Army and the Navy and a programme of social reform. Perhaps, however, the most telling epithet for this group is the description of them as Radical Authoritarians. They had no interest in freedom or democracy or the rule of privilege; rather, they wished for a meritocracy run by a great leader with the Empire as the chief focus of the State. They believed that the people could be won over to support imperialistic objectives and the ties forged with the masses could circumvent party machines and leaders. Arthur Balfour, the Prime Minister, in particular became the but of their discontent, with his languid style '. . . airy graces . . . subtle dialectics, and . . . light and frivolous way of dealing with great questions' he epitomized for them the flabby leadership which the Salisbury 'dynasty' had given to the Conservative Party for too many years.[31] It had totally failed in the eyes of the men of the Radical Right to elicit the instinct of patriotism that existed in the nation as a whole.

'The Sons of Martha', therefore, can be seen as an attempt to channel popular feeling against what Kipling and other adherents of this group deemed to be the elite that was in charge of Britain in the Edwardian years. However, although the tariff reform campaign of Chamberlain and that for conscription by Lord Roberts can be seen as real efforts to recompose the power bloc, Kipling's lines were moralistic rather than programmatic. They were a complaint that those in positions of power were passive and lazy, a complaint that England was led by the wrong people. This stress on leadership was typical of many populist responses and it appeared in fuller and perhaps more alarming detail in 'Things and the Man'.[32]

Dated 1904 and published in *The Times*, these verses bore the dedication 'In Memoriam Joseph Chamberlain'. However, they mourned not his death, but his resignation from the Conservative government and the increasing difficulty he was having by August 1904 in sustaining the momentum of the tariff reform movement that he had set up on his departure from the House. Once again the poem inverted the ultimate outcome of the Biblical incident cited at the outset. The reference was to the passage in Genesis about Joseph's dream which, of course, after trial and tribulation was fulfilled. Chamberlain's dream was to win support from the nation for protectionism via extra-parliamentary activity that would force the political parties to reconsider their attitude towards what he regarded as the 'shibboleth' of free trade.

'Things and the Man' suggested that this dream would remain exactly that – a dream. The use throughout of the past tense in the refrain, '*Once upon a time there was a Man*', besides giving the impression that Chamberlain's moment had already passed, also gave the verses the air of a lament and a very bitter one at that. While, however, the lines admitted that Chamberlain was unlikely to be successful, and in doing so recognized also the strength of the tradition of Parliamentary government in Britain, the detestation of this system was by no means compromised or elided. It was stressed unrelentingly that the country's salvation still lay in recognizing the great leader in its midst:

> Thrones, Powers, Dominions block the view
> With episodes and underlings –
> The meek historian deems them true
> Nor heeds the song that Clio sings –
> The simple central truth that stings
> The mob to boo, the priest to ban;
> *Things never yet created things* –
> '*Once on a time there was a Man*.'[33]

The dismissal of the historian as the one least likely to be able to heed the Muse of History was typical both of Kipling's anti-intellectualism and that of the populist tradition with which these views can be associated. The distrust of institutions and organizations was complete: '*Things never yet created things*'. A nation's power depended upon the great leader, only through him might the people 'grip the purpose of his plan'. There was in these lines the historical analysis of Seeley, 'unto him [Chamberlain] an Empire clings', the belief that that was where Britain's future lay, its pre-eminence could only be secured through its economic and political unity.[34] The poem foresaw also the kind of authoritarian state that Matthew Arnold had envisaged. Strenuousness of the most individualistic and vigorous sort typified the Chamberlain who appeared there:

> He, single-handed, met and slew
> Magicians, Armies, Ogres, Kings.
> He lonely mid his doubting crew –
> "In all the loneliness of wings" –
> He fed the flame, he tilled the springs,
> He locked the ranks, he launched the van
> Straight at the grinning Teeth of things.
> '*Once on a time there was a Man*.'[35]

The language here describes Chamberlain dispensing the old order with the industrial instruments of the new and later in the poem he appears in equally god-like proportions putting to pay tradition and false reverence with expert intelligence:

> The peace of shocked Foundations flew
> Before his ribald questionings.
> He broke the Oracles in two,
> And bared the paltry wires and strings.[36]

The dream had been a country ruled by a reformed and revived aristocracy of leadership of the type that Carlyle had always demanded. Nevertheless, although the dream was located in the past and was looked back on with some nostalgia, the penultimate line of the poem deliberately set out to relocate the issues it had raised in the present. It asked: 'My Lords, how think you of these things?'[37] The specific direction of the question to 'Lords', most probably the 'Diehard' contingent of the Upper House, who thought in terms very similar to those of the Radical Right, must have reminded many other members of the Establishment that the Kipling of 'The Islanders' was still very active. Verses like this and 'The Sons Of Martha' showed that there existed in England at this time a group on the right wing who constituted a threat, not only to the Conservative Party but to the constitution of the country, in that they were able to foresee possibilities of national reordering and reconstruction by other than parliamentary or party political means.

This preference for a strong leader who was not to be found among the traditional political groupings seems to have been redirected towards Edward VII after Chamberlain's stroke in 1906. What, however, is significant in terms both of our understanding of Kipling's position and the mood of the radical right wing in these years is that the poem was addressed to another leader of great worth who had not achieved his ends. 'The Dead King' is again a lament that might suggest to us now that those who held these views recognized, even if they did not admit it, the ultimate defeat of their position: in more ways than the obvious one, many of the verses in this collection, while fiercely adhering to and defending their own principles, were also elegiac. Published on 18 May in British and US newspapers, 'The Dead King' mourned the passing of Edward VII in 1910.[38] Though never known, until his later years for any reverence towards royalty, Edward had appeared to Kipling and many others as a man bred for his time, who in his diplomatic activity proved willing to lay 'down dear life for the sake of a land more dear!'.[39] He was praised in these verses for those qualities that the Radical Right valued in particular and felt were absent from Conservative politics then; the King's ability, for instance, to forge ties with the people so that they eagerly responded with patriotic instincts:

> In the clear-welling love of his peoples that daily
> accrued to him,
> Honour and service we gave him, rejoicingly fearless;
> Faith absolute, trust beyond speech and a friendship
> as peerless.[40]

What seems to have appealed most, however, was the monarch's capacity to recognize and promote merit:

To him came all captains of men, all achievers of glory,
Hot from the press of their battles they told him their
  story
They revealed him their life in an hour and, saluting
  departed,
Joyful to labour afresh – he had made them new-hearted.
And, since he weighed men from his youth, and no lie
  long deceived him,
He spoke and exacted the truth, and the basest believed him.[41]

Apart from this vision of a nation unified in the community of interest one man was able to encompass, the lines also exalted the world of practicality and action that was actively encouraged during Edward's reign by the Co-Efficients formed in 1902. Although Kipling was never one of their offical number, the emphasis in these verses, and in a story like 'Below the Mill-Dam', shows that he like they saw England's well-being as depending upon a lead in the business affairs and technology of the new century.[42] King Edward had been famous for his disregard for social rank; his friendship with Sir Thomas Lipton, 'the grocer', was famous and annoyed the many who still despised position that was earned from commerce. The concern of these lines was, however, not egalitarian in any way at all; rather, Edward was used as an example of a leader who recognized, as Chamberlain had, that opportunities of interest and advantage must be seized in order to make it possible for Britain to survive in a world of future rivalry and conflict in which the race would be won by the swift and the prize would go to the strong. However, the source of the power of the great leader and of the activity of the captains of industry and commerce was, as ever, the Empire – this was the 'Ark' that had been 'borne to Zion'.[43]

In the verses that spoke of imperial matters, the note struck again was one of bitterness and anxiety and the time was foreseen when 'The Pro-Consuls' would be openly rejected by the dependent Empire:

Doubted are they, and defamed
  By their tongues their act set free,
While they quicken, tend and raise
Power that must their power displace.[44]

The Empire now was a cause of worry rather than satisfaction, but although, like the British State, it was deemed to be in need of radical overhaul, these poems offered no political strategy. Once more the approach was moralistic. Repeatedly, the lines sought to inspire shame in politicians who 'squandered. . . . The strength and glory of our reputation' and to arouse xenophobic feelings within the average reader.[45] 'The Rowers', published in *The Times* on 22 December 1902, was a strident outburst against England's joining with Germany to blockade Venezuela to force the government to pay its debts. An editorial observed that it 'expressed sentiments which unquestionably prevail far and wide throughout the nation'.[46] The lines drew upon the fact that Germany's ambitions in Africa and its support for the Boers were fresh in the public's mind, so that their representatives, the British sailors who spoke in the poem, railed against being the servants of what seemed a fickle and opportunist policy:

> Last night you swore that our voyage was done . . .
> And you tell us now of a secret vow
> You have made with an open foe.

But this political complaint was laced with a racist attack that still appears neurotic in its virulence. The 'cheated crew' spoke out against being leagued 'With the Goth and the shameless Hun'.[47] By returning the Germans to their medieval and tribal origins, Kipling was, obviously, able to assuage his own well-known loathing of this country and its people. He was also able, given that they would have had many readers in common, to enhance and probably increase the hatred of Germany that Leo Maxse whipped up every month in the *National Review*. Both men were adept at a propagandist type of writing which, specifically, targeted their victim and unequivocally told people what to think. Certainly, the Kaiser was vexed by the behaviour of the British press and particularly resented Kipling's contribution 'as hitherto he had been a great admirer of that individual's work'.[48] 'The Rowers' played upon the fears that many people had about Germany's European and imperial ambitions, which, it was argued, made her the least suitable of allies for England. The real complaint that lay behind the xenophobia and anger of both these members of the Radical Right was that England had never learnt to be an imperial nation, it had never understood that the acquisition of territory brought with it the price of constant vigilance and defence, in short military preparedness.

However, the refusal to assume the identity fate had thrust upon it was in these Edwardian years preached to the young as well. A poem written for the volume of school history he produced with C.R.L. Fletcher stressed the need to be militaristic and alert to the dangers of soft living, because enemies were always awaiting the moment when the guard might drop:

> If war were won by feasting,
> Or victory by song,

Or safety found in sleeping sound
  How England would be strong!
But honour and dominion
  Are not maintained so,
They're only got by sword and shot
  And this the Dutchmen knew.[49]

In more moderate and certainly less histrionic tones, these lines told youth in 1911 what their elders had received via newspapers and journals throughout the previous decade. And this was not the only effort to disseminate his views more widely across the nation. Kipling was in close contact during these years with Lord Roberts, whose campaigns he had seen in India and had played a small part in in South Africa. On his return, Roberts had formed the National Service League and stomped the country arguing the need to introduce universal service and training for home defence to free the Regular Army for its commitments in other parts of the globe. Kipling's story 'The Army of a Dream' was written to draw attention to and support this cause. It was published first in the *Morning Post* between 15 and 18 June 1904 and shortly afterwards in *Traffics and Discoveries*. It was then re-issued separately and sold to the public at 6d a copy in November 1905.

This publishing history occurred simultaneously with some of Lord Roberts's most passionate expositions of his theme. At the same time as Kipling's story was issued in pamphlet form, Roberts declared that 'none of the leading politicians seem to realise the necessity for making any serious effort to render our army capable of meeting demands that may suddenly come upon it'.[50] Two greatly revered figures, therefore, were heard loudly and in many different places hammering the issue 'on the anvil of the electorate'.[51] The support they gained over the years was by no means negligible, massive numbers would go to hear both men when they made public speeches. By 1909, *The Times*, *Daily Telegraph*, *Daily Mail* and the *Spectator* all gave them their backing. However, they were subjected to a flow of abuse from the left-wing press and in 1908 Roberts had received from the King a memorandum asking him not to raise the question of Germany. In the lines written in memory of Lord Roberts, who died in 1914, inspecting troops on the Western Front, Kipling noted that:

The weighed and urgent word
That pleaded in the market-place –
  Pleaded and was not heard![52]

In *The Years Between*, therefore, there was a significant change in the political tenor of the verses. Prior to this collection, the ideas and attitudes expressed in the verse could be associated quite legitimately with the broad sweep of Victorian Conservatism. Now, however, there was the deliberate adoption of a style that was prophetic of the death of the nation, repeatedly the spectre with which the reader was tormented was that of 'headlong surrender' and the reversal of Biblical passages of hope and affirmation gave a particularly bitter flavour to the portents that were interpreted.[53] There was a complete absence of humour from this volume and the stress placed on the need for a powerful leader, the necessity for the organization of the state on military lines and the disdain for traditional forms of government all suggested a radical form of authoritarianism that went beyond the bounds, certainly of Parliamentary rhetoric as well as that of indigenous political debate. The most lurid verses were yet to come, however, in response to the constitutional crisis that preceded the war and to some of the events of the war itself.

Since the ending of the Boer War, the Radical Right and many Unionists had pinned their hopes on the Tariff Reform campaign as the last hope of launching a popular imperial movement that would reconstruct conservatism and the state. However, the Liberal landslide at the polls in 1906, and Chamberlain's stroke in that year too, had made this seem increasingly unlikely. Between 1906 and 1909, the Liberals, first led by Campbell-Bannerman and then Asquith, attempted to introduce a series of social reforms that included an Education Bill, a Trade Disputes Bill to reverse the Taff Vale judgment and a Plural Voting Bill. There was a good deal of Unionist rhetoric about the revolutionary, socialistic nature of these measures, though they were in fact reformist in the classic nineteenth-century pattern. There was no central planning or direction and they tinkered, often successfully, with social problems, but at no point were these dealt with at root. On the imperial front, independence was granted to the Transvaal, and in India the Morley-Minto Reforms made the legislative councils, hitherto nominated, at least partially elective and increased their scope. The strategy Balfour used to delay and obstruct these Liberal measures was in the short term effective, though later it threatened the unity of the party that he sought to preserve. The massive majority held by the government in the Commons meant that little could be achieved there by debate. In the Lords, however, the Conservatives were in the majority, so, as a general rule, Bills were allowed to pass easily through the Lower House, only to be held up or savaged in the Upper House.

Lloyd George's budget first presented on 29 April 1909 destroyed this strategy, eventually broke the impasse of Edwardian party politics and in so doing drastically altered the political landscape and the fortunes of the Radical Unionists. A total of £16 million was required if the

Chancellor was to finance the scheme for old-age pensions that the government had proposed back in January 1909, and the answer to the problem came in the form of the radical clauses in Lloyd George's budget, that included Death Duties, Super Tax and a Land Tax. The reactions of the Unionists were immediate and intense. Balfour condemned it as 'vindictive, inequitable, based on no principle and injurious to the productive capacity of the country'.[54] From his sick-bed, Chamberlain inveighed against it too; and Carson saw it as 'the beginning of the end of all rights of property'.[55] Years later, looking back on these times, Lloyd George was not disposed to minimize the danger which had faced government and country:

> We were beset by an accumulation of grave crises – rapidly becoming graver. . . . It was becoming evident to discerning eyes that the Party and Parliamentary system was unequal to coping with them. . . . The shadow of unemployment was rising over the horizon. Our international rivals were forging ahead at a great rate. . . . Our working population were becoming sullen and discontent. . . . A great Constitutional struggle over the House of Lords threatened revolution at home.[56]

In this situation, 'The City of Brass', published in the virulently sectarian *Morning Post* of 28 June 1909, sought to inflame Unionist response against both the so-called 'People's Budget' and the Liberal government to date.[57]

Like many of the other poems, the note struck appeared to be elegiac; it mourned 'lost dominion', not however, with sadness and resignation, but with apoplectic rage that might be sufficiently contagious to produce in like-minded readers a similar reaction against this abdication of power which was also a denial of national identity. The danger invoked was seen to be perilously near: by the end of the verses Britain had 'passed from the roll of nations' and its going was apocalyptic – 'Out of the sea rose a sign – out of Heaven a terror.' As in the Biblical last days, 'the heart of a beast in the place of a man's heart was given . . .' and the poet's voice was that of the prophet seeking to warn and arouse Britain against such a fate. The Liberals were caricatured as seeking 'To decree a new earth . . . without labour and sorrow':

> They said: "Who is eaten by sloth? Whose unthrift has
>   Destroyed him?
> He shall levy a tribute from all because none have
>   employed him."
> They said: "Who hath toiled? Who hath striven, and
>   gathered possession?

> Let him be spoiled. He hath given full proof of
> transgression."[58]

Income tax, pensions and labour exchanges were identified, in all likelihood quite correctly, as an attempt to create an active and popular basis for Liberalism, by giving 'to numbers the Name of Wisdom unerring'. Chamberlain had for many years championed old-age pensions and Kipling and others on the right were willing to sanction social reform, as long as it was a means of gaining popular support for imperial policy. The Liberal Party, however, had made social reform part of a regime that allowed 'more pay for the shouters and marchers'. It would lead, eventually, to 'the impregnable ramparts of old' being 'razed and relaid'.[59]

'The City of Brass' claimed to behold an ideological shift on which Lloyd George had sought to capitalize with his radical measures. These measures were destructive of the very qualities that were essential in an imperial nation. They impugned 'Faith and Endeavour', they 'exposed to derision / All doctrine of purpose and worth and restraint and prevision'. Capitalist enterprise was under threat, the energy that drove the commercialism of *The Seven Seas* would no longer be revered, but dissipated in contempt. It was not merely that the Empire had not grown since the Boer War, but despite the Tariff Reform League and Chamberlain's exertions, Hobson's and Morley's views had gained ground, the idea that '. . . the show and the word and the thought of Dominion is evil!' had become more widespread. Behind the hysteria of these verses, therefore, lay the suspicion that there was now an ideological complex whose *modus vivendi* was the casting off of 'The imperial gains of the age which their forefathers piled them.'[60] The Empire would be dismantled at a blow, Churchill had already spoken of making self-government for the colonies 'the gift of England' and in events in South Africa and India was the evidence that 'they awakened unrest for a jest. . . . They instructed the ruled to rebel' and then 'Praise[d] the upheaval!'[61]

The prospects held out by 'The City of Brass' left the Unionist who was associated with the Radical Right no alternative but to reject the budget and rebel against the government. This the Lords did and, deprived of finance, the Liberals found it impossible to govern. This situation then became a confirmation of the view promoted in other verses that the system at Westminster was no longer adequate to cope with domestic and imperial issues. Simultaneous direct action by trade unionists and insurgent feminists, which also produced the most belligerent and provocative statements by Kipling, made it seem that popular politics too was escaping the control of the parliamentary system. In

1911, the suffragettes had developed new methods of violence and in November of that year came the riposte that has provided the English language with a catchphrase. Again it was published in the *Morning Post*, on 20 October 1911.[62] As Blanche points out, a key feature of imperialist ideology was its strikingly connotative male character and the continuous pressure that the suffragettes had exerted throughout society to make their presence felt surely provided a threat to the patriarchal leadership models on which imperialism so often depended.[63] As the poem made perfectly clear, women had throughout history challenged the authority of the father:

> When the early Jesuit fathers preached to Hurons
> and Choctaws,
> They prayed to be delivered from the vengeance of
> the squaws,
> 'Twas the women, not the warriors, turned those
> stark enthusiasts pale.
> For the female of the species is more deadly than
> the male.[64]

The poem comprised 13 stanzas in this vein and each 'worked' in exactly the same way; the woman was a figure of excess, ruthless, immune to justice and without conscience. A creature of instinct, 'who may not govern', she was represented as a threat to the manhood of the race. She could be an obstacle to male achievement, certainly she was the source of that which was alien in his world, 'She the Other Law we live by, is that Law and / nothing else.'[65]

It was, however, in verses about the political situation in Ireland, which were also saturated in masculinism, that hysteria reached a climax and became incitement to rebellion, to a rejection of the Constitution. In January 1912, the Home Rule Bill was proceeding slowly through the House of Commons and it had provoked a militant backlash from the Unionists in the north of Ireland, who were desperate to resist at all costs the end of their union with the United Kingdom. Accordingly, on 5 January 1912, Ulstermen began to drill volunteer forces. The Radical Right saw the secession of Ireland as the first stage in the dismantling of the Empire so that their cause was very much one with Ulster. Whereas the Liberal Party sought to resolve the crisis through concession and negotiation, the views expressed in 'Ulster' reveal that Kipling and those like him looked for some catastrophic resolution to the problem. The poem was published in England in the *Morning Post* of 9 April 1912 and separately in New York and Belfast as well as at Ulster Unionist Headquarters.[66] It was released on this date to coincide with the salute taken by Carson, Lord Londonderry, Bonar

Law and Walter Long of some 80,000 Orange Volunteers. There was no ambiguity in the position represented in the verses; they contained the same icy determination that Carson exhibited in his speeches on the subject. 'By England's act and deed', Ulster was being 'sold':

> To every evil power
> We fought against of old.

And as:

> The dark eleventh hour
> Draws on . . .

only one response was possible:

> What answer from the North?
> One Law, one Land, one Throne.
> If England drive us forth
> We shall not fall alone.[67]

These lines aimed to heighten antagonism and to rearrange the basic elements of the political situation by a reversal of associations. The government was linked with 'Murder . . . Treason . . . folly, sloth and spite', whereas those urging insurrection and defiance of Parliament bore all the qualities of true manhood: loyal to 'flag and throne' they accepted with staunchness, sobriety and discipline that 'We are the sacrifice', and, in doing so, of course, tried to rally more to their ranks. The potency of such verse can perhaps be gauged when it is realized as part of the larger situation in which, on both sides, passions were rising to a dangerous level. At a Unionist rally in July, Bonar Law, now leader of the Opposition, had declared that:

> I can imagine no length of resistance to which Ulster can go in which I should not be prepared to support them, and in which, in my belief, they would not be supported by the overwhelming majority of the British people.[68]

Later in the speech he added, 'I said the other day in the House of Commons, and I repeat here, that there are things stronger than Parliamentary majorities.'[69] Like 'Ulster', these statements encouraged defiance of constitutional conventions. Coming from the leader of a political party and a well-known writer, they were threats of treason and armed rebellion, they looked towards civil war and are indicative of the nature of the role they sought to play in a profound political crisis, the magnitude of which did not merely affect party policy but the very foundations of the country's political institutions.

When in 1914 the crisis over Ireland seemed to be about to erupt into civil war, Kipling was campaigning even more fiercely in a manner unlikely to have encouraged any peaceful solution to the problem. On 15 May, he made a speech at Tunbridge Wells that was published by the *Daily Express*. Called 'Rudyard Kipling's Indictment of the Government', it was sold for 1d at the news stalls and by street vendors, so that it was well within the financial reach of the passer-by. A day later came an address to the League of British Covenanters called 'The Secret Bargain, the Ulster Plot'; this time it was the *Morning Post* that reprinted it and sold it for a 1d. 'The Covenant', written 6 days later, converted the war-like rhetoric into verse.[70] It was first published in *The Convenanter*, a paper whose sole reason for existence was to express Unionist allegiance to British imperialist ideology and it appeared 2 days later, on 22 May 1914, in *The Times* and the *Daily Telegraph* as well. It is doubtful whether any other verse by an English writer has ever secured such a wide-ranging readership at a crucial moment in the development of an affair.

'The Covenanter' was written to coincide with the passage of the Home Rule Bill again through the Commons, and it threatened that whatever might be decided there by the 'Merchants in freedom' there would remain 'His Mercy' that would be 'sought / Through wrath and peril till we cleanse the wrong'. Since the Curragh Mutiny earlier in March had revealed that the Army's loyalty was not total, this prophecy of civil insurrection must have appeared at the time as a very real threat.[71] Small wonder perhaps that Asquith commented that Unionist rhetoric portended 'an absolute end to Parliamentary Government' and 'a complete grammar of anarchy'.[72] Churchill, not yet converted to populist opportunism, described the Ulster Volunteer Force as 'treasonable conspiracy' and saw the nation threatened by a few malcontents.[73] The verse in this volume may have been 'neglected' by the literary critics, but the wide exposure it had received on its first publication had ensured that it contributed to the crisis of parliamentary politics in the Edwardian period and it aligned with those who were willing to contemplate civil war as a way of realigning, in a more satisfactory way, British political institutions.

It was, therefore, perhaps inevitable that when war was declared the situation in which the nation found itself should be represented in some verses as the end result of the 'headlong surrender' in which it had indulged for too long. Many of the poems written throughout the war years were excessive in the way that 'The Female of the Species', 'Ulster' and 'The Covenant' had been. Among these one might include 'Justice', 'The Question', 'The Verdicts' and, the most unpleasant of them all, 'A Death Bed', which revelled in the pain and suffering of the Kaiser as he died from cancer of the throat.[74] The brush strokes of these poems were broad and their colours bright, the tone of them all was belligerent and often vitriolic. German government and people, for example, appeared before the British public in 1914 as 'The Outlaws', who for years had been plotting 'Fresh terrors and undreamed of fears / To heap upon mankind.' Their gross immorality, their failure to be bound by international law, was to be seen in their behaviour towards Belgium: they 'utterly laid waste a land / Their oath was pledged to guard'. However, the intention behind the verses, the role they sought to play in forming national opinion, can only be understood by paying attention to the final verse:

> They paid the price to reach their goal
>   Across a world in flame;
> But their own hate slew their own soul
>   Before the victory came.[75]

Here was an assurance of German defeat, that evil such as theirs could not prosper in this world. Certainly, the reader can find in this narrow view the one-sidedness and limited sense of values that has irked many of our own contemporaries who have written about the poetry of the First World War and Kipling's response to it. None of the verses written during the war included either reference to or sympathy for the enemy's suffering and there were some that revelled in the possibility of increasing it. In 'The Song of the Lathes', published in February 1918, a woman, as usual, proves the most vengeful of 'the species' when, after the deaths of her husband and son in Flanders, she works in a munitions factory where her great satisfaction is to '*Feed the Guns*'.[76] As Silkin has noted, '. . . reconciliation was never in Kipling's vocabulary'.[77] In the 1920s, he renewed his warning about the German menace and declared that 'those memories of the dead . . . They have been burned into us forever'.[78] Charles Hamilton Sorley's observation that in fact Britain and Germany were sisters in their approach to politics and their outlook on life was a perception that never entered Kipling's verse.[79]

What should be added, however, is that literary-cum-moral judgements of this kind restrict our historical perspective on the formation of the national consciousness during these years. Furthermore, by failing to distinguish these verses from those of the soldier poets, they confuse a civilian response with theirs and they fail to attend to the nature of that civilian response. Literary critics, indeed most people, might prefer to judge the attitudes incorporated in this verse as indefensible, but in doing so they are choosing to ignore those popular attitudes, often quite contradictory, which produced the national will that maintained the political will that saw Britain through the war. Kipling was one with the nation in 1914 in not being anti-war. Between 1914 and 1918, crushing military defeats were many and quite monstrous in the loss of human life, and yet they did not prove decisive; that this should have been so indicates that there remained a political will to resist. The most insignificant of military engagements can be decisive if the political will to continue is exhausted. Political will, however, is not simply about the resolve of politicians, it is also a reflection of national morale. Maintenance of this is perhaps the most important element in the success of modern war. To be correctly understood, the verse of these years has to be seen as participating in the production of this national morale, and however much 'the average humane reader' might regret it now, the atavistic emotions that Kipling sought to arouse were constituents of the national will that 'won' the war. Until mid-1917, the mobilization of public opinion in England was left to individuals. As time went on, however, and casualties on the Western Front reached ever vaster proportions and a greater number of people became involved in the war effort, it became increasingly clear that public opinion could not be ignored: its attitudes and moods played a vital part in the way the people conducted themselves in relation to the war. Kipling was often approached to make speeches and write to support the national cause and a good number of the verses mentioned so far bear many of the characteristics of propaganda, they 'dealt with the war in such a way as to propagate the cause of the one side and discredit that of its opponents'.[80] To this end, some of the verses provided a simple image of the enemy, they made it absolutely clear what people should think about him and they had a certain if biased knowledge of their target.

Not all of the verse written during this period was, however, of this type, although one critic has suggested that 'For All We Have & Are' was of this class. It is, he claims, a call to arms which relishes the onset of the War.[81] This is, however, to assert a single-mindedness that the poem does not show, it blurs the actual differences between the kinds of poems by Kipling that were written at this time, but perhaps most importantly of all it suggests the naivete of the nation: that at a turning point of history it responded with no more than simple-minded flag-waving, for this poem was published widely in British and American newspapers on 2 September 1914. Rather, there is in 'For All We Have & Are' a recognition of something the historian J.M. Bourne has emphasized, which is the corollary of an understanding of the importance in wartime of public opinion, that '. . . all modern wars are fought on two fronts. The home front is not only as important as the war front but also inseparable from it.'[82]

References to the Hun and to a 'world . . . passed away, / In wantonness o'erthrown' might seem to support Bergonzi's view and be a reminder of the obsessive preoccupations of earlier work. But in this poem, these black and white distinctions exist alongside a consideration of the nature of the war about to be fought and what it will mean for youth and its parental generation. The effect is a diffusion of meaning that allows it to touch on many of what we now know were characteristic responses to the declaration of war and, no doubt, to draw in more readers to the commonalty of feeling that the lines tried to build. There is, for example, the acceptance of national destiny that characterized popular response as it welcomed the news of war; that at such a moment 'There is but one task for all', that the war must be 'taken', it was necessary in order to defend civilized values.[83] At the same time, these verses did not disguise the terror and awful prospect of the forthcoming conflict. While Brooke, Grenfell and Sassoon were glorying in the redemptive aspects of battle, the war represented here had more in common with the Hebraic perspective one finds in Rosenberg:

> Once more we hear the word that sickened earth of old –
> "No law except the Sword
> Unsheathed and uncontrolled."
> Once more it knits mankind.[84]

As well as being the punishment for a crime, 'to break and bind / A crazed and driven foe', war is in itself a crime. In this contradictory position, the war as necessary and war as a peculiarly vile human activity is the same disparity one notes in much behaviour during these years. For example, the enthusiastic and patriotic mass of volunteers was, by September 1914, singing unpatriotic marching songs. The one thing does not belie the other and the same is true of Kipling's poem.

Neither do the lines provide a heroic gloss on the deaths that will inevitably occur. The answer to the question 'Who dies if England live?' was not hard to seek when the newspapers carried pictures on a daily basis of young men queuing up to enlist, and this final line of the poem reminds the reader of earlier phrases in it which take on added meaning: 'Though all we knew depart . . . Though all we made depart'. These refer not only to a way of life, but also to the soldiers leaving for the Western Front. This is 'our children's fate' invoked in the first line of the poem. The implications for both children and parents is carried further in the direct address to the latter. The older generation are warned of the coming days and the only comfort it will have is a stoic resignation, 'In patience keep your heart'. The poem predicts an actuality that occurred only too soon, an England emptied of young men, where:

> Only yourselves remain
> To face the naked days
> In silent fortitude.

The renewal that was looked for was to be found in resistance that demanded of both soldiers and civilians:

> . . . iron sacrifice
> Of body, will and soul.[85]

Wilfred Owen, as late as 1917, suffering 'the merciless iced east winds' and the tension and monotony of trench warfare, was to claim that, although the men fighting were now broken by their experiences, no more than ghosts of their former selves, no longer able to find a home where they once had, nevertheless they turned back to their dying on the Western Front:

> Since we believe not otherwise can kind fires burn;
> Nor ever suns smile true on child, or field, or fruit.
> For God's invincible spring our love is made afraid;
> Therefore, not loath, we lie out here; therefore were born,
> For love of God seems dying.[86]

Through the suffering, the scepticism and the metaphysical questioning comes a continuing commitment to go on, 'to survive Prussia'.[87] The commitment of both writers to resistance in the face of the shock and strain of war, the point at which men break, indicates a common feeling and understanding in soldier and civilian that ultimately bound the nation together. Owen, of course, in some of his letters and his revered poem 'Strange Meeting', indicated another position that was pacifist and internationalist; and by 1917 there were many at home in England who were doubting whether the price of so-called victory had not been too high. However, the poets fought on and the nation continued its war effort and in the contradiction between thought/feeling and behaviour lay the similarity and strength of the relationship between home and fighting front. The interest of 'For All We Have & Are' lies in its containment and realization of these contradictions in national attitudes which, in these years, did not negate or belie one another. The condemnation of the verses as 'facile and pretentious' tells more about the political hostility between Kipling and the liberal intelligentsia that Orwell noted than it does about the way the British people felt and thought as the war was about to begin.[88]

There are other poems, too, in this collection that have received little or no critical attention but which reveal much about the nature of national feeling as it experienced the sorrow incurred by the fighting. Some of these verses show that the differences between the common preoccupations and concerns of those in England and those in the Army were inevitable because of the generation gap and the anxieties that imposed. Alongside Sassoon's angry indictment of generals and their staff, or Owen's accusation about the 'Insensibility' of politicians, one might set Kipling's poem 'Mesopotamia', a tirade against a campaign in which 23,000 died relieving a force of 13,000 that found itself under siege because of poor leadership.[89] Sassoon strikes his effect through comic satire, Owen with a scathing contempt that points to the tragedy of a whole generation of young men, Kipling in the tones of the Biblical prophet expresses the bitterness of those whose sons have been 'Coldly slain' and he cries for vengeance when the war is over. All of them are concerned with incompetence of one sort or another, with the disempowerment of the individual absorbed by the military machine and then '. . . left . . . thriftily to die in their own dung'.[90]

However, the soldier poets are able to reclaim their individuality and their dignity in their awareness of what is being done to them. They speak, 'Knowing that there is no reward, no certain use / In all [their] sacrifice', and in this existential defiance their 'honour is reprieved', they strive to rise above the national interests and the individuals who are to blame for their situation.[91] To civilians responding to the same situation existential defiance was not really a possibility. Given that their response was produced by their concern for those on active service, they had no wish to accept the meaninglessness of the conflict or the inevitability of the death of those they loved. Left to wait and worry, they could not solace themselves with the comradeship of the trenches or with having led men well. All they could do was watch stoically as those whose incompetence had caused so many deaths 'sidle back to power . . . confirm and re-establish their careers'.[92] It is a truism now to remark on the way modern warfare reduces the soldier to a passive victim of his own destiny, but it is important to note that civilians too experienced an increasing feeling of helplessness as the war proceeded. A helplessness made more bitter by the inaccessibility of politicians and military leaders to censure and, despite all the improvements in communications, by their distance from their loved one. 'Mesopotamia' is very much a product of this situation, although it is powerful public rhetoric, throughout it can only repeat the same circle of negative emotions and, in the end, it becomes the victim of its own corrosive bitterness and frustration.

A few other poems in this collection, not written for the public occasion, participate in their own way, from a peculiarly civilian point of view, in the same kind of metaphysical questioning that is so often present in Owen, and they concede, albeit inadvertently, the meaninglessness of the conflict. 'A Nativity' and 'My Boy Jack' have as their subject the grief and mourning of parents for their sons lost in battle.[93] The first two of these poems are similar in that they both evoke the terrible anguish of mothers whose sons are 'missing presumed dead' and each poem tries to end convincingly on an affirmative note, asserting that comfort is to be found in the knowledge that their boy 'did not shame his kind'.[94] However, these affirmations are undercut by the prior content of the poems.

'A Nativity' works in the same way as 'Dedication' and 'The Sons Of Martha': it plays upon a Biblical parallel whose meaning is inverted by showing the excess of the contemporary comparison. So, the mother in this poem sees her son's manner of death as exceeding the cruelty of that handed out to Christ and her own role as more demanding than that of Mary. After all, Christ's Mother:

> . . . saw Him die
> And took Him when He died
> Seemly and undefiled.[95]

However, the soldier's mother knows 'not how he fell', nor 'where he is laid'. His shattered body could have lain for days with 'none to tend him'. The awfulness of Calvary, therefore, is overtaken by the monstrosity of the Western Front. Mankind has outdone itself in barbarism, so that the question that becomes a refrain, 'Is it well with the child, is it well?', with its heavy falling emphasis on the word 'well', finds no meaningful answer despite the affirmative assertion that follows.[96] The missing body on Easter Day, that was a sign of the risen Christ, is deliberately set against the missing body of the soldier, which is a sign that he is lost forever: meaningful death is set against a meaningless death. The lines imply that no Christian interpretation can explain the fate of the 'children' in this war.[97] Mankind has passed beyond the bounds of Christian explanation and inhabits a world where there is no meaning, no 'Sign of the Promise given'. The assertion at the end of the poem that 'all is well with the child' only heightens the poignance that this is certainly not so.[98] It is a claim for well-being in the face of overwhelming odds against it. Whereas in 'For All We Have & Are' the doubt and affirmation did not belie one another, this is no longer true – here religious and metaphysical principles are in turmoil.

A similar process occurs in 'My Boy Jack', which had been included in *Sea Warfare* in 1916. The final injunction to 'hold your head up all the more' in pride at the sacrifice of the son lost at sea this time, comes after the reader has received a strong impression of minimal meaning. Whereas this arose in 'A Nativity' through the contrast with Christ, in this poem the refrain creates the effect. The repetition of the elemental ferocity of 'this wind blowing and this tide' ensures that 'news of my boy Jack' becomes an ever-decreasing possibility. By the end of the poem, the refrain has come to represent the monstrous powers that in this war are destroying mere boys, and the fact that Jack 'did not shame his kind' heightens their awfulness and the tragedy of his loss.[99]

'Gethsemane', which deliberately recalls Christ's passion in the garden, is the only poem in this collection in which we hear the voice of the ranker.[100] But, it is a ghostly voice from the dead, and the fate he describes, in which he can play no active role, suggests that the earlier chirpiness of 'Tommy Atkins' is forever lost to Army life. The parallel with Christ, much used by the front line poets, is used here to different effect. Readers are directed not so much towards the sacrifice and suffering of the soldiers, but towards the fact that the appeal of both that their 'Cup might pass' was never answered and that maybe they inhabit an empty world, without meaning, 'beyond Gethsemane'. What all three poems indicate is that although the home fires were being kept burning during these years, although there was a common fund of attitudes that made for a cohesive war effort, nevertheless the same question asked by Wilfred Owen in 'Futility' was also on the lips of civilians:

> Was it for this the clay grew tall?
> – O what made fatuous sunbeams toil
> To break earth's sleep at all?[101]

Despite the plethora of literary criticism about the poetry of the First World War and also the large number of anthologies containing it, very little attention has ever been paid to Kipling's final poetic statement on the subject – a sequence entitled merely 'Epitaphs'. One of the reasons no doubt arises from a judgement about war poetry that is still accepted as a truism: that the brevity and the subjectivity of the lyric made it unsuitable for representing the magnitude of the war. The epic it is claimed was the only form that could have incorporated such large vistas and produced the necessary appreciation of the total experience of war. Once this line of argument is accepted, it is inevitable that the 'Epitaphs' will be dismissed as attempting, in their minuscule form, the impossible. Kipling's failure once more to conform to the dominant mode expected of poetry of a certain type becomes an argument for neglecting it and, inevitably, therefore, denying it any critical attention. Ironically, however, because of the brevity and the swift changes of location, mood and subject that they allow, the 'Epitaphs' do convey an impression of the cultural and geographical magnitude of the war and they encompass a whole range of reactions and attitudes which have to be included in any attempt to understand the nation's experience of war. The starting point for the whole act of memorialization is:

Equality of Sacrifice
A I was a "have" B I was a "have-not"
(TOGETHER) What hast thou given that I gave not?[102]

This emphasis on the classlessness of death is then brought to a sharp focus in social terms:

A Servant
We were together since the war began,
He was my servant – and the better man.[103]

The variety of voices that speak throughout – 'The Ex-Clerk', 'The Refined Man', etc – makes it clear to the reader that one of the strongest impressions produced by the war on soldiers and civilians was that historic, cultural and class divisions had been laid aside. It is an insight into the bitterness and incomprehension of those who returned to find the fabric of English society unchanged and unchanging. Furthermore, the respect and reverence accorded 'The Hindu Sepoy' and 'The Native Water-Carrier' contained no reference to the self-government India hoped for in repayment for this heavy service. And, in more ways than this, things were unchanged.

The politicians and politics so heavily castigated in the pre-war verse stand again condemned, with their 'lies proved untrue' as they now face the ultimate arbiter of the future years: 'mine angry and defrauded young'.[104] Indeed, 'The Common Form' of the 'Epitaphs' tells the reader:

If any question why we died,
Tell them that our fathers lied.[105]

However, something Kipling wrote 2 years later does not suggest that he included himself among those whom the young would regard as guilty. Writing on 'England & the English' he said, 'through the first two years of the war it was necessary to throw-up a barricade of the dead bodies of the nation's youth behind which the most elementary preparations could be begun'.[106] The blame was back with the Liberals for not listening to the militaristic and authoritarian solutions that he and others like him had proposed.

Even within this ideological framework, however, another kind of effect arises from the stress on 'equality of sacrifice'. The reader is moved quickly through brief lives in ever-widening geographical dimensions. There are references to naval engagements, graves near Cairo, Halfa and Salonika and the effect is to extend the reader's awareness beyond the Western Front to the most far-flung battlefields of this war. The reader commits to memory not only poignant details about the fallen, but becomes the witness of a new historical phenomenon – the first *world* war. Individual and family tragedies are captured in details made more pitiful by the terseness with which they are expressed: the young boy who died on his first day in the trenches because curiosity got the better of him and he peeped out only to be hit by the sniper's bullet; or the only son whose death broke his mother's heart. But, the attention is drawn also to other kinds of instances and reactions: to those who found purpose and courage in the war and those who had committed the most vengeful crimes. Certainly, 'The pity of war' is 'distilled' through these instances, whose poignance is heightened by our knowledge that there were 73,000 similar ones on the British side alone.[107] However, the wide vista encompassed by the sequence forces an encounter too with what seem to be ultimate contradictions – a world and a humanity that is simultaneously ennobled and brutalized. As so often in the prose, in this collection, the metaphysical underpinnings of political confidence seem scanty and desperate.

Some of the verses here, therefore, maintained an equipoise within the contradictions of national feeling, but others tested out traditionally held beliefs and in doing so exposed the gap between ideology and everyday experience. Despite its unswerving and unchanging political position, there were in the collection verses capable of producing parodic meaning, especially in relation to Christian values and beliefs. These verses evaded the ideological thrust of these beliefs and turned their norms back on themselves. In this sense, *The Years Between* deserved to be the most neglected of all Kipling's collections by what Orwell termed the 'liberal intelligentsia', challenging as it did the political traditions of the country and the literary, religious and metaphysical limits of the still dominant liberal outlook.

Conclusion: 'A Good Bad Poet'

No more new collections of verse appeared after *The Years Between*, though Kipling continued to command space in the quality and popular press.[1] A 'plebiscite' held in 1913 by the *Journal of Education* to try to establish the names of the most popular poets showed Kipling as the leader, followed by William Watson, Robert Bridges and Alfred Noyes.[2] Various compilations of verses from earlier collections were also published and sold extremely well; however, although many individual poems were published singly, they were only collected in the successive *Inclusive Editions* of his work that appeared during his lifetime in 1919, 1921, 1927 and 1933.[3] A *Definitive Edition* was published in 1940 on the authority of his daughter and it is the edition which remains in print to this day.

Kipling was himself responsible for the order of the verses in the *Inclusive Editions* and in most instances he used it to confirm the view of British history that had been presented and re-presented from 1899 onwards. So, for example, the reader finds 'The Lesson' (1902), with its hope that the revelations of the Boer War 'may make us an Empire yet', succeeded immediately by 'Mesopotamia' (1917), with its call for revenge upon 'the idle-minded overlings' and 'The shame that they have laid upon our race.' Predictably, this is followed by 'The Veterans' and 'The Dykes'. Apart from a final section, the chronological order in which the verses were written is ignored in favour of a highly flavoured version of history that sometimes hisses with hatred and rage and at other times pours vitriolic contempt upon a nation that has sold its heritage: 'we have slain our sons, as our fathers we have betrayed'.[4]

The conclusion to the *Definitive Edition* provided by the 'Miscellaneous Verse' draws the attention of the reader to the folly that was still perceived to be going on.[5] In the place of the Liberals stand the Socialists who 'daily tarnish' the 'Faith, Obedience, Sacrifice, / Honour and Fortitude!' of those who had truly understood Disraeli's observation that 'a nation is a work of art and time'.[6] 'The Storm Cone', written in 1932, and published first in the *Morning Post* and then in separate editions, anatomized the momentum of what was seen to be the inevitable crisis that such policies would produce:

> This is the tempest long foretold –
> Slow to make head but sure to hold
>
> Stand by! The lull 'twixt blast and blast
> Signals the storm is near not past;
> And worse than present jeopardy
> May our forlorn to-morrow be.[7]

Such verses must have reminded members of both literary and political institutions that what Le Gallienne had said in 1919 continued to be true, 'lovers of the best in literature . . . have never quite learned to like Rudyard Kipling. There is something in him that still frightens them.'[8] However, the way in which critics since these times have reproduced the views of the nineteenth-century literary establishment requires the reader of today to identify what the source of the fear was and still is.

George Orwell, perhaps, provides the most interesting and detailed example of the posthumous critical response to Kipling's verse.[9] In one sense, he saw to the heart of the matter when he noted the apparent contradiction between the 'fact' that Kipling's verse could appear to some 'morally insensitive' and 'aesthetically disgusting', while enjoying enormous popularity with far many more. How could verse that was 'so horribly vulgar that it gives one the same sensation as one gets from watching a third-rate music-hall performer' nevertheless appeal to 'the intellectual and the ordinary man' like a 'shameful pleasure?'.[10]

In answering this question, however, Orwell merely repeated and perpetuated the judgements that construct and maintain the gulf between popular writing and literature. Even at his best, Orwell argued, in verse like 'Mandalay', Kipling lacked the clarity and measure of a traditional ballad such as 'Felix Randal' and he certainly could not match the lyric sweetness of Shakespeare's song, 'When icicles hang by the wall'.[11] In comparisons of these sort, literary value does not reside in the text but in the valuer, who, for particular reasons, sets store on the differences between one text and another.

A similar kind of thinking emerges in Orwell's response to Kipling's dialect poems. Full of 'snack-bar wisdom' and 'cheap picturesqueness', they contain 'some emotion which very nearly every human being can share'.[12] However, this kind of universality was not it seems worthy of praise because 'popular poetry is usually gnomic and sententious' and its 'stage cockney dialect was irritating'. A final condemnation was provided when Orwell declared that the dropped aitches made some very ugly sounds.[13] Such an observation about poetry typifies the obsessive concern of a certain kind of literary criticism with a value that relates not to the ideological matrix of his/her own reading, or that of the text's production, but to some abstract notion of original thought and civilized speech against which the popular stands condemned as 'vulgar' and 'spurious'.[14] Indeed, the conclusion that Orwell came to might seem odd in a critic who had accused Kipling of being unaware of the class war. Orwell declared that 'the mere existence of work of this kind, which is perceived by generation after generation to be vulgar and yet goes on being read, tells one something about the age we live in'.[15] There is very little distance here between him and those reviewers who had seen Kipling's verse as the inevitable and deleterious product of a debased publishing institution required to cater for a more socially various and literate electorate.

This book began with the issue as set out by Harold Orel: that Kipling's work poses:

> . . . one of the most serious problems in modern criticism, the relationship between members of the Establishment . . . and writers who, for one reason or another, do not seem to satisfy the Establishment's expectations of what they *should* be saying . . .[16]

In terms of political ideology, it is not difficult to understand how Kipling's verse had and might continue to offend an Establishment which still includes members with inherited wealth and position, as well as some who adhere to Liberal and Socialist values. The continuing currency of their position and, perhaps, the commentary of the verse on it, in a historical conjuncture perceived by many to be one of terminal national decline, maintains the acidity and pointedness of the satire, even if a reader has little sympathy with what are seen to be remedies.

In terms of Kipling's literary relations, it is now possible to see that at the root of the problem Orel identified is the threat that Kipling's verse posed from the outset to definitions of the literary that remain dominant to this day. His whole poetic discourse was at variance with most of the poetry that was being written in his own time – in terms of form, content and language. The lyric was ignored, the political and social were central, and dialect and vituperation provided the oratorical means of expression. Such a body of work still remains today outside that produced by the majority of British contemporary poets. The exception perhaps is a poet who writes from a quite different ideological standpoint, but who, in a poem like 'V', has sought the effect Kipling strove for in a poem like 'The Islanders'.[17]

Tony Harrison has described his writing as a 'quest for a public poetry'. Such a quest, he says, 'prefer[s] the idea of men speaking to men to a man speaking to god, or even worse to Oxford's anointed'.[18] This kind of poetry finds its audience in those places where most men venture most frequently – in the marketplace, the newspaper or on television – rather than in the study or the seminar room. Orwell had identified the characteristics of 'good bad poetry', but had preferred not to speculate about its potential and the implications that might have. One of its most significant characteristics that he noted was its ability 'to get across the most unpromising audiences' and give 'pleasure to people who can see clearly what is wrong with it'. This was, he admitted, 'a sign of the emotional overlap between the intellectual and the ordinary man'.[19] Should this overlap be deliberately sought by writers, the way would be open for a poetry that actively eroded the very distinctions which separate good from bad poetry. Literature and the elitest values on which it rests might be contested and redefined.

It is not surprising, therefore, that verse with such a potential should be considered a literary anomaly and outlawed as vulgar. Whether it comes from the left or the right it bears with it the possibility of influencing significantly the areas of exchange between classes where hegemonic leadership is won. Moreover, it should be added that literary distinctions of this kind are a question of politics not aesthetics. In its own time, Kipling's verse was part of the attempt by a powerful group to reorganize culture so as to enclose it within an inclusive imperial nationalism that sought to create a semblance of unity across class and party lines. Perhaps it is no coincidence that another group of radical right-wing politicians who have, since the late 1970s, sought to produce a new hegemony within all the institutions of this country, should have had as its favourite poet, Kipling, the one writer who struggled in his work to achieve discourses that crossed the social formation and roused and unified the nation.

Notes

Introduction

1 Harold Orel, 'Rudyard Kipling and the Establishment: A humanistic dilemma', *South Atlantic Quarterly*, LXXXI, 1982, p. 162.
2 No book-long study of Kipling's poetry exists to date. The essays that have been written about it are much fewer in number than the critical works on his prose writings.
3 After 1919, new verses had an initial appearance in the Press and sometimes as pamphlets, and then went into the several *Inclusive Editions* of Kipling's work. This is dealt with more fully in the Conclusion.
4 W.T. Stead, *Review of Reviews*, 15 April 1899. Spencer's article is cited here; see Benita Parry, *Delusions and Discoveries*, 1972, Ch. 6, pp. 202–203.
5 T.R. Henn, *Rudyard Kipling*, 1967, pp. 75–6.
6 Orel, op. cit., note 1, p. 166.
7 Penguin Books and Oxford University Press. Macmillan still publish their hardback and paperback editions of Kipling's complete works.
8 Lacan, quoted in M. Bowie, *Freud, Proust and Lacan: Theory as Fiction*, 1987, Ch. 5, p. 158.
9 Tony Bennett, 'Texts in history: The determinations of readings and their texts', in D. Attridge, G. Bennington and R. Young (eds), *Post-Structuralism and the Question of History*, 1988, pp. 70–71. See also A. Parry, 'Reading formations in the Victorian periodical press: The reception of Kipling 1888–1891', *Literature and History*, 11(2), 1985, pp. 254–63.

Chapter 1: 'Official Sinning'

1 T.S. Eliot, 'Introduction', in *A Choice of Kipling's Verse*, 1941, p. 7.
2 E. Said, *Orientalism*, 1978; B. Parry, *Delusions and Discoveries*, 1972;

B. Anderson, *Imagined Communities*, 1983; H. Bhaba, *Nation and Narration*, 1990; J.M. McKenzie (ed.), *Imperialism and Popular Culture*, 1986; J.M. McKenzie (ed.), *Propaganda and Empire*, 1984.

3 *Definitive Edition* (hereafter *DE*), 1982, pp. 3–82.

4 L. Cornell, *Kipling in India*, 1966, p. 41.

5 'Christmas in India', *DE*, p. 56.

6 Edward Farley Oaten, *A Sketch of Anglo-Indian Literature*, The Le Bas Prize Essay, 1908, pp. 177, 181.

7 'Pink Dominoes', *DE*, pp. 18–19.

8 The phrase is used in the last verse of 'A General Summary', *DE*, p. 4.

9 R. Kipling, 'My first book', *McClure's Magazine*, 3(6), November 1894, p. 564.

10 Ibid.

11 Ibid.

12 *DE*, pp. 21–2.

13 B. Martin Jr, *New India 1885: British Official Policy and the Emergence of the Indian National Congress*, 1969, p. 10.

14 C. Eldridge, *England's Mission: The Imperial Idea in the Age of Gladstone and Disraeli 1868–1880*, 1973, p. 226.

15 Ibid.

16 'The Indian Delegates', in A. Rutherford (ed.), *Early Verse by Rudyard Kipling 1879–1889* (hereafter *EV*), 1986, pp. 296–7.

17 E. Dicey, 'Mr Gladstone and our Empire', *The Nineteenth Century*, 11, September 1877, pp. 292–308.

18 'A General Summary', *DE*, p. 4.

19 W.E. Gladstone, 'Aggression on Egypt and Freedom in the East', *The Nineteenth Century*, 11, August 1877, pp. 149–66.

20 Ibid., p. 164.

21 Speech at Leeds, 7 October 1881, quoted by P. Magnus, *Gladstone: A Biography*, 1954, p. 287.

22 Eldridge, op. cit., note 14, p. 6.

23 'Trial by Judge', *EV*, p. 291.

24 R.J. Moore, *Liberalism and Indian Politics 1872–1922*, 1966, p. 59.

25 F. Hutchins, *The Illusion of Permanence: British Imperialism in India*, 1967. Hutchins argues that in the second half of the century, India became the last hope and resort of reactionaries. Those who went there were likely to be men excited by the desire to rule rather than reform, concerned with British not Indian hopes. There is vindication for this suggestion in Kipling's work. In 'One Viceroy Resigns', Dufferin remarks to Lansdowne:

> I followed Power to the last,
> Gave her my best, and Power followed me
> It's worth it.

In 'The Judgement of Dungara' (1888), Gallio's motives for imperial service also strike a chord with Hutchin's argument: 'He was a knockneed shambling young man, naturally devoid of creed or reverence with a loving for absolute power which his undesirable district justified.'

26 Quoted in L. Wurgaft, *The Imperial Imagination*, 1983, p. 24.
27 Salisbury to Disraeli, 7 June 1876, *Salisbury Papers*, Christ Church Library, Oxford.
28 *DE*, pp. 69–73.
29 *EV*, p. 294.
30 Anderson, op. cit., note 2, p. 136. Ashis Nandy discusses phobic racism in *The Intimate Enemy: Loss and Recovery of the Self Under Colonialism*, 1981.
31 'A New Departure', *EV*, pp. 184–5.
32 'In the Case of Rukhimbhaio', *EV*, pp. 373–5.
33 *EV*, pp. 278–9.
34 Dufferin to Halifax, January 1885, cited in Moore, op. cit., note 24, p. 50.
35 Moore, op. cit., note 24, pp. 43–8. Kipling's own service in the Punjab made him aware of what he deemed another threat to English power, that of Russia beyond the frontier. He records the importance and cost of policing this area in heroic terms in 'Arithmetic on the Frontier', *DE*, p. 45.
36 C. Philips (ed.), *The Evolution of India and Pakistan 1858–1947: Select Documents*, 1962, pp. 138–9.
37 Moore, op. cit., note 24, p. 51.
38 'Delilah', *DE*, p. 7.
39 Martin, op. cit., note 13, p. 19.
40 *DE*, p. 17
41 *DE*, p. 14.
42 *DE*, pp. 15–17.
43 *DE*, p. 17.
44 Quoted in R.L. Green (ed.), *Kipling: The Critical Heritage*, 1971, p. 12.
45 A phrase from *Vanity Fair*, quoted by M. Edwardes, *The Sahibs and the Lotus*, 1988, p. 195.
46 'Public Waste', *DE*, p. 14.
47 D. Kincaid, *British Social Life in India*, 1939, p. 230; the remarks by Younghusband are quoted in Angus Wilson, *The Strange Ride of Rudyard Kipling*, 1977, p. 112.
48 Kipling, op. cit., note 9, p. 564.
49 *DE*, pp. 69 and 35 respectively.
50 Green, op. cit., note 44, pp. 34–5.
51 Ibid., p. 34.
52 Ibid., p. 35.
53 B. Moore-Gilbert, *Kipling and Orientalism*, 1986, argues that Anglo-Indian discourse in the post-Mutiny era lived in tension with that of the metropolitan. Such an argument is well supported by 'Pagett MP' and Kipling's own statements in *Something of Myself* (1937). However, it fails to account for the satire of the *Ditties and Other Verses* manifestly directed against Anglo-India.
54 'Pagett MP', *DE*, pp. 26–7.
55 Eldridge, op. cit., note 14, p. 213, cited from *Hansard*.
56 *DE*, p. 27.

57 Ibid., p. 27.
58 Ibid., p. 78.
59 Said, op. cit., note 2, p. 3.
60 *DE*, p. 78. H.J. Field's *Toward a Programme of Imperial Life: The British Empire at the Turn of the Century*, 1982, is in general interesting on character-building, as are also several essays in McKenzie's collections.
61 *DE*, p. 78.
62 The review is partially quoted in Green, op. cit., note 44; see W.W. Hunter, 'Departmental Ditties & Other Verses', *The Academy*, 3, No. 852, September 1888, pp. 128–9.
63 'To the Address of WWH', *EV*, p. 404.
64 'One Viceroy Resigns', *DE*, p. 73.
65 Hunter, op. cit., note 62, p. 128.
66 *DE*, p. 8.
67 Hunter, op. cit., note 62, p. 128.
68 Ibid., p. 128.
69 Ibid., p. 129.
70 *DE*, p. 74.
71 *DE*, pp. 54–6.
72 Hunter, op. cit., note 62, p. 129.
73 Ibid., p. 128.
74 *DE*, p. 4.
75 *DE*, pp. 35–9.
76 *DE*, pp. 36–7.
77 *DE*, p. 39.
78 Kipling, *The Day's Work*, 1987, pp. 131–64, tells us of the superhuman work done by District men and women during a famine.
79 *EV*, p. 468.
80 'The Rupaiyat of Omar Kalvin', *EV*, pp. 25–6.
81 Ibid., p. 25.
82 C. Eldridge (ed.), *British Imperialism in the Nineteenth Century*, 1984, pp. 65–84.
83 Hunter, op. cit., note 62, p. 128.
84 *DE*, pp. 69–70.
85 *DE*, pp. 70, 72.
86 *Athenaeum*, 1, April 1890, pp. 527–8.
87 Ibid., p. 527.
88 *DE*, p. 28.
89 F. Adams, 'Mr Rudyard Kipling's verse', *Fortnightly Review*, 60(OS), November 1893, pp. 590–603.
90 'The Tale of Two Suits', *EV*, p. 275. On the *Bungalow Ballads*, see Cornell, op. cit., note 4, pp. 83–5.
91 *DE*, p. 12.
92 'Inscriptions in Presentation Copies of Echoes', *EV*, pp. 250–51.
93 *DE*, p. 3. At certain points throughout his life, Kipling was to proclaim his oneness with Anglo-India (e.g. *Something of Myself*). Also, however, as he settled down at Bateman's in Sussex, he concentrated in his

writing on defining a sense of place and spirit that was essentially English, especially in 'Puck of Pook's Hill' and 'Just so Stories'. These alternating preoccupations suggest, perhaps, the ambivalence of his response to both.

94 Verses from 'A Letter to Andrew Lang', *EV*, pp. 467–9.

95 'What the People Said, Queen Victoria's Jubilee, June 21, 1887', *DE*, pp. 66–7.

96 See, for example, R. Shannon, *Crisis in British Imperialism 1865–1915*, 1974; B. Porter, *The Lion's Share*, 1975, esp. Ch. 4; R. Hyam, *Britain's Imperial Century*, 1976, esp. Chs 3 and 4.

Chapter 2: 'Missis Victorier's Sons

1 *Barrack-Room Ballads & Other Verses*, Methuen Centenary Edition, 1989, flyleaf.

2 C.E. Norton, 'Kipling's poetry', *Atlantic Monthly*, LXXIX, January 1897, quoted from R.L. Green (ed.), *Kipling: The Critical Heritage*, 1971, p. 187.

3 See, for example, W.W. Hunter, 'Departmental Ditties & Other Verses', *The Academy*, 3, No. 852, September 1888, pp. 128–9; 'Review of Soldiers Three', *The Spectator*, 23 March 1889, pp. 403–404.

4 ' "Kipling About" in London for a Week by a Hustling American', *Kipling Journal*, 7, October 1928, pp. 9–16.

5 *Something of Myself*, 1937, p. 69.

6 A.B. Maurice, 'Kipling's verse people', *The Bookman*, 9, March 1899, pp. 57–61.

7 *Something of Myself*, p. 69; *EV*, p. 468.

8 *Something of Myself*, p. 70.

9 'The Widow at Windsor', *DE*, pp. 413–14.

10 Maurice, op. cit., note 6, p. 59.

11 W.E. Henley, 'Concerning Atkins', *Pall Mall Magazine*, XXI, 1900, pp. 280–83.

12 Hunter, op. cit., note 3, *The Academy*, p. 128.

13 Hunter, op. cit., note 3, *The Spectator*, p. 403.

14 Hunter, op. cit., note 3, *The Academy*, p. 128.

15 Mowbray Morris had been art director of the *Pioneer* for a while.

16 T.W. Heyck, *The Transformation of Intellectual Life in Victorian England*, 1982, p. 20. The price of Kipling's work in these early days would have placed it beyond the means of all but the middle and upper classes.

17 *Something of Myself*, p. 63.

18 Diana Howard, *London Theatres and Music-Halls 1850–1950*, 1970; see also Kipling's letters about his music-hall memories and enthusiasms in J.B. Booth, *The Days We Knew*, 1943.

19 Kipling tells us that he paid 4d for entry into Gatti's music hall and had also for this price a pint of porter. Historians of the music hall suggest that this would be the lowest entrance fee for the less fashionable halls. See

P. Bailey (ed.), *Music-Hall: The Business of Pleasure*, 1986, esp. D. Hoher, 'The composition of music-hall audiences 1850–1900'. Gatti's was a very small music hall: 'The space between the stalls, instead of being wide, as it is at the Canterbury, is extremely cramped, and the seats remind one of those at an ancient coffee-house'. ('The state of the London music-halls, No. 2', *The Saturday Review*, 20 August 1887, pp. 255–6.

20 J. Ewing Ritchie, *Days and Nights in London*, 1880, p. 53.
21 *Something of Myself*, p. 68.
22 Kipling, 'My Great & Only', in *Abaft the Funnel*, 1907, p. 262.
23 Ibid., p. 270.
24 Ibid., p. 269.
25 Ibid., pp. 271, 273
26 G. Steadman-Jones, *Languages of Class: Working-Class Culture and Working-Class Politics in London 1870–1900*, 1983, pp. 179–238.
27 Ritchie, op. cit., note 20, p. 40.
28 F. Adams, 'Mr Rudyard Kipling's verse', *Fortnightly Review*, 60(OS), November 1893, pp. 590–603; M. Schuyler, *Forum*, 22 December 1896, pp. 406–413.
29 *Something of Myself*, p. 63; 'My Great & Only', in *Abaft the Funnel*, p. 265.
30 P.J. Keating, *The Working Classes in Victorian Fiction*, 1971, p. 165.
31 A. Quiller Couch, 'Reviews and reminders: On some living English poets', *English Illustrated Magazine*, X, No. 120, September 1898, pp. 901–903.
32 *DE*, p. 398.
33 *Illustrated London News*, 19 January 1889, pp. 83–4; 2 February 1890, p. 139; see also 15 February, 15 March, 12 and 19 April, 17 and 24 May, and 7 and 14 June 1890.
34 T.H. Ward, *The Reign of Queen Victoria*, 1887; B. Bond, 'The late Victorian army', *History Today*, XI, 1961, 616–25; E. Spiers, *The Army and Society*, 1980.
35 'Cells', *DE*, p. 404.
36 'Gentleman-Rankers', *DE*, p. 424.
37 *Hansard*, 3rd series, Vol. 350, col. 1143, 1889.
38 'Shillin' a Day', *DE*, p. 429.
39 'Rudyard Kipling the poet', unsigned review, *London Quarterly Review*, 178(59), January 1898, pp. 325–36.
40 J.S. Bratton, *The Victorian Popular Ballad*, 1975, esp. pp. 74–88.
41 J.B. Booth, *Old Pink 'Un Days*, 1924, pp. 397–8.
42 *Hansard*, 3rd series, Vol. 341, col. 1350, 27 February 1890.
43 *DE*, p. 398.
44 *DE*, p. 413.
45 *DE*, p. 398.
46 *DE*, p. 410.
47 *DE*, p. 397.
48 *DE*, pp. 397–8.
49 *DE*, p. 412.

50 *Illustrated London News*, 19 January 1889, 'The Relief of Suakin, Charge of the 20th Hussars', p. 91; 9 March 1889, 'Sketches of Suakin'.
51 *DE*, p. 400.
52 *DE*, p. 234.
53 *DE*, pp. 400–401.
54 *DE*, p. 413.
55 *DE*, p. 418.
56 *DE*, pp. 418–20.
57 *DE*, p. 419.
58 *DE*, p. 419.
59 Schuyler, op. cit., note 28, p. 407.
60 Adams, op. cit., note 28, p. 597.
61 *DE*, p. 83.
62 *DE*, pp. 83–4.
63 *DE*, p. 406.
64 *DE*, p. 394.
65 *DE*, pp. 394–5.
66 *DE*, pp. 238, 243.
67 *DE*, p. 250.
68 *DE*, p. 250.
69 *DE*, p. 255.
70 *DE*, p. 332.
71 Couch, op. cit., note 31, p. 902.
72 *DE*, p. 255.
73 *DE*, p. 255.
74 *DE*, p. 243.
75 *DE*, p. 234.
76 *DE*, p. 400.
77 *DE*, p. 221.
78 *DE*, p. 250.
79 *DE*, p. 284.
80 *DE*, p. 284.
81 *DE*, p. 284.
82 Norton, quoted in Green, op. cit., note 2, p. 187.
83 'Political Anthropology', quoted in P. Stallybrass and A. White, *The Politics and Poetics of Transgression*, 1986, p. 14.
84 *DE*, p. 419; 'Troopin' ', p. 420; 'Mandalay', p. 419; 'Gunga-Din', p. 406.
85 'Fuzzy-Wuzzy', *DE*, p. 401.
86 The first reference is to R. Stamm, 'On the Carnivalesque', in Stallybrass and White, op. cit., note 83, p. 19; the second is to Adams, op. cit., note 28, p. 597.
87 Norton, quoted in Green, op. cit., note 2, p. 187.
88 Stallybrass and White, op. cit., note 83, p. 16.
89 T. Eagleton, *Walter Benjamin*, 1981, p. 148; Stallybrass and White, op. cit., note 83, p. 13.
90 R. Shannon, *Crisis in British Imperialism 1865–1915*, 1974, pp. 12–13.
91 On the matter of/speculation about personal phobias, see Ashis Nandy,

The Intimate Enemy: Loss and Recovery of the Self Under Colonialism, 1983.

Chapter 3: 'So long as The Blood endures'

1 'The works of Mr Kipling', *Blackwood's Magazine*, 164, October 1898, p. 474.
2 C.E. Norton, 'The poetry of Rudyard Kipling', *Atlantic Monthly*, LXXIX, January 1897, p. 113.
3 'England's Answer', *DE*, p. 178.
4 Op. cit., note 1, p. 474.
5 Ibid., p. 471.
6 'The Widow at Windsor', *DE*, p. 413.
7 'Mr Kipling's new ballads', *The Spectator*, 77, 21 November 1896, p. 728.
8 *DE*, p. 179.
9 *DE*, pp. 170–71.
10 'Rudyard Kipling the poet', unsigned review, *London Quarterly Review*, 178(59), January 1898, p. 333.
11 'The Lost Legion', *DE*, p. 195.
12 'The Coastwise Lights', *DE*, p. 172.
13 'The Song of the Cities', *DE*, p. 176.
14 'The Merchantmen', *DE*, p. 153.
15 R. Shannon, *Crisis in British Imperialism 1865–1915*, 1974, p. 221.
16 Ibid., p. 225.
17 Ibid., p. 218.
18 J.L. Garvin, *The Life of Joseph Chamberlain, Vol. 3: 1895–1900, Empire and World Policy*, 1934, p. 68.
19 C. Carrington, *Rudyard Kipling: His Life and Work*, 1986, p. 283.
20 C. Eldridge, *Victorian Imperialism*, 1978, pp. 204–206 on 'The Anglo-Boer War'.
21 Garvin, op. cit., note 18, p. 67.
22 B. Porter, *Britain, Europe and the World 1850–1982: Delusions of Grandeur*, 1983, pp. 56–81 on 'Crisis 1895–1914'.
23 *DE*, pp. 66–7.
24 See Chapter 2 for a further discussion of these points.
25 *DE*, p. 328.
26 *DE*, p. 194.
27 Porter, op. cit., note 22, p. 61.
28 A.M. Gollin, *Pro-Consul in Politics*, 1964, p. 130.
29 H. Browne, *Joseph Chamberlain: Radical Imperialist*, 1974, p. 52.
30 C.W. Boyd (ed.), *Mr Chamberlain's Speeches*, 1914, Vol. 2, 'The true conception of empire: To the Royal Colonial Institute, March 31, 1897', p. 5.
31 Ibid., p. 5.
32 Garvin, op. cit., note 18, p. 27.
33 *DE*, p. 170.

34 *DE*, p. 170.
35 A. Milner, *The Nation and the Empire*, 1913, a collection of speeches from the past decade, quoted in E. Crankshaw, *The Forsaken Idea*, 1952, p. 121.
36 *DE*, pp. 171–2.
37 Ibid.
38 *DE*, pp. 172–3.
39 *DE*, p. 172.
40 *DE*, p. 172.
41 *DE*, p. 172.
42 *DE*, p. 173.
43 *DE*, pp. 173–4.
44 *DE*, p. 173.
45 *DE*, p. 196.
46 *DE*, p. 170.
47 *DE*, p. 192.
48 *DE*, p. 192.
49 *DE*, p. 175.
50 *DE*, p. 175.
51 *DE*, p. 178.
52 Garvin, op. cit., note 18, pp. 187–8.
53 Ibid., p. 188.
54 Ibid., p. 188.
55 Ibid., p. 191.
56 Ibid., p. 193.
57 K. Jones, *Fleet St and Downing St*, 1919, pp. 145–9.
58 H.O. Arnold Forster, *The Citizen Reader: For Use in Schools*, 1904, pp. 13–14.
59 Walter Besant, *The Rise of Empire*, 1897, p. 2.
60 Walter Besant, 'Is it the voice of the hooligan?', *Contemporary Review*, LXXVII, 1900, pp. 29–39.
61 J.A. Hobson, *Imperialism: A Study*, 3rd edn, 1938, p. 101.
62 R. Price, *An Imperial War and the British Working Class*, 1972 and 'Society, status and jingoism: The social roots of lower middle class patriotism 1870–1900', in G. Crossnick (ed.), *The Lower Middle Class in Britain 1870–1914*, 1977.
63 J.M. McKenzie (ed.), *Imperialism and Popular Culture*, 1986, p. 6.
64 R. Roberts, *The Classic Slum*, 1971; see also McKenzie, op. cit., note 63, pp. 5–6.
65 S. Humphries, *Hooligans or Rebels?*, 1981, p. 41.
66 *DE*, p. 442.
67 *DE*, pp. 455–7; 'Mary Pity Women' appears in the German version of Brecht's *Threepenny Opera*.
68 Norton, op. cit., note 2, p. 115.
69 Quoted by J.B. Booth in *The Days We Knew*, 1943, p. 39. See Penny Summerfield, 'Patriotism and empire: Music-hall entertainment 1870–1914', in McKenzie, op. cit., note 63, pp. 17–48.

70 Garvin, op. cit., note 18, p. 27.
71 Lord Rosebery, *Questions of Empire*, 1900, p. 23.
72 *DE*, p. 329.
73 E. Said, *Nationalism, Colonialism and Literature: Yeats and Decolonisation*, Field Day Pamphlet No. 15, 1988, pp. 6–7.
74 *DE*, p. 180.
75 *DE*, p. 180.
76 'Song of the Dead', *DE*, p. 174.
77 'Song of the English', *DE*, p. 170.
78 'The Native Born', *DE*, p. 194.
79 Porter, op. cit., note 22, p. 64.
80 R. Buchanan, 'The voice of the hooligan', *Contemporary Review*, LXXVI, December 1899, pp. 774–89, in R.L. Green, *Kipling: The Critical Heritage*, 1971, p. 247.
81 Carrington, op. cit., note 19, p. 282.
82 *DE*, pp. 325–6.
83 Buchanan, in Green, op. cit., note 80, p. 247.
84 *DE*, p. 325.
85 *DE*, p. 179.
86 *DE*, pp. 176–7.
87 *DE*, p. 172.
88 *DE*, p. 451.
89 *The Spectator*, 77, 21 November 1896, p. 728.
90 A.C. Benson, *Life of Edward White Benson Sometime Archbishop of Canterbury*, 1899, p. 133.
91 Garvin, op. cit., note 18, Vol. 1, see pp. 548–58 on unauthorized programme.
92 'Some minor poets', *London Quarterly Review*, 186, October 1897, p. 327.
93 *DE*, p. 126.
94 *DE*, p. 133.
95 *DE*, pp. 98–101.
96 'Sestina of the Tramp Royal', *DE*, p. 87; 'For to Admire', *DE*, p. 457.
97 *DE*, p. 88.
98 *DE*, p. 458.
99 'Dedication', *DE*, p. 179; 'When 'Omer Smote Is Bloomin' Lyre', *DE*, p. 351.
100 *DE*, pp. 444–6.
101 Shannon, op. cit., note 15, p. 221.
102 *DE*, p. 454.
103 *DE*, p. 455.
104 *DE*, pp. 451–3.
105 B. Anderson, *Imagined Communities*, 1983, p. 136.
106 *DE*, p. 451.
107 *DE*, p. 452.
108 Buchanan, in Green, op. cit., note 80, pp. 241–2.
109 *DE*, p. 430.

110 Buchanan, in Green, op. cit., note 80, p. 237.
111 Ibid., p. 235.
112 Ibid., p. 238.
113 Ibid., p. 242.
114 Op. cit., note 1, p. 473.

Chapter 4: 'Before a Midnight Breaks in Storm'

1 See James Morris, *Farewell the Trumpets: An Imperial Retreat*, 1979, p. 71.
2 E. Dowden, 'The poetry of Mr Kipling', *New Liberal Review*, XXVIII, February 1901, pp. 53–61. These references are taken from R.L. Green, *Kipling: The Critical Heritage*, 1971, p. 259.
3 See Chapter 1, p. 29.
4 Quoted in R. Faber, *The Vision and the Need: Late Victorian Imperialist Aims*, 1966, p. 99.
5 Ibid., p. 36.
6 R. Koebner and H.D. Schmidt, *Imperialism: The Story and Significance of a Political Word 1840–1960*, 1964, esp. Ch. 8, 'The incorporation of Africa into the imperial idea and the climax of popular imperialism', pp. 196–220.
7 Antonio Gramsci, 'The Intellectuals', in *Selections from the Prison Notebooks*, 1971, p. 10.
8 Ibid., p. 10. Kipling's involvement in activities that supported the Boer War are well covered in Carrington, *Rudyard Kipling: His Life and Work*, 1986, Ch. 13; see also J.S. Galbraith, 'The pamphlet campaign on the Boer War', *Journal of Modern History*, XXIV(2), June 1952, pp. 111–26.
9 Angus Wilson, *The Strange Ride of Rudyard Kipling*, 1977, p. 213.
10 'The Dykes', *DE*, pp. 305–307.
11 *DE*, p. 104.
12 *DE*, p. 106.
13 *DE*, p. 270.
14 Faber, op. cit., note 4, p. 108.
15 Ibid.
16 *DE*, p. 182. Kipling wrote to Moberley Bell, the editor of *The Times*, 'I WANT the papers to quote it like anything. The more the merrier. Please let 'em!'; see Tom Pinney (ed.), The *Letters of Rudyard Kipling*, 1990, Vol. 2, p. 296.
17 *DE*, p. 183.
18 Faber, op. cit., note 4, p. 75.
19 *DE*, p. 183.
20 Pinney, op. cit., note 16, Vol. 2, pp. 308–309.
21 *DE*, p. 287.
22 Koebner and Schmidt, op. cit., note 6, p. 217.
23 J.McK. Robertson, *Wrecking the Empire*, 1901, p. 208.
24 Faber, op. cit., note 4, p. 84.
25 *National Review*, 6, p. 251.

26 Carrington, op. cit., note 8, p. 337.
27 See Carrington, op. cit., note 8, pp. 408–409, for the offence it caused in the USA.
28 *DE*, p. 323.
29 *The Times*, 18 January 1899, quoted by S. Koss, *The Pro-Boers*, 1973, p. xix.
30 Ibid., p. xix.
31 G.P. Gooch, *Liberalism and Empire*, 1901, p. 138.
32 F. Harrison, 'The evolution of our race: A reply' (review of K. Pearson's *National Life and Character*), *Fortnightly Review*, 60, 1894, pp. 28–41.
33 *DE*, p. 324.
34 *DE*, p. 198.
35 *DE*, p. 203.
36 *DE*, p. 204.
37 *DE*, pp. 204 and 199.
38 H.R. Marshall, 'Kipling and the racial instinct', *Century*, 58(3), July 1899, p. 376.
39 *DE*, p. 141.
40 *DE*, p. 145.
41 *DE*, pp. 296–8.
42 *DE*, pp. 296–8.
43 Hugh Cunningham, 'The language of patriotism 1750–1914' *History Workshop Journal*, 12, 1981, pp. 8–33.
44 *DE*, p. 298.
45 See J. McKenzie (ed.), *Imperialism and Popular Culture*, 1986 and *Propaganda and Empire*, 1984.
46 S. Koss, *The Rise and Fall of the Political Press in Britain*, 1990, pp. 373–4.
47 Francoise Pressense, *Contemporary Review*, LXXV, February 1899, pp. 158–60.
48 Koss, op. cit., note 46, pp. 368–9.
49 R. Price, *An Imperial War and the British Working Class*, 1972.
50 Kipling, *Something of Myself*, 1937, p. 113.
51 Wilson, op. cit., note 9, p. 213.
52 T.S. Eliot, *A Choice of Kipling's Verse*, 1963, p. 18.
53 *Something of Myself*, p. 113.
54 J. Gross (ed.), *Rudyard Kipling: The Man, His Work and His World*, 1972, p. 84.
55 Collected in Kipling, *Abaft the Funnel*, 1907; see Chapter 2, pp. 35–46.
56 *DE*, pp. 459–60.
57 Price, op. cit., note 49, p. 5.
58 *DE*, p. 460.
59 *Daily Mail*, 23 October 1899.
60 These figures are taken from the essay by M.D. Blanche, 'British society and the war', in P. Warwick (ed.), *The South African War: The Anglo-Boer War 1899–1902*, 1980, see pp. 214–15.
61 *DE*, p. 468.

62 *DE*, p. 459.
63 Howard Bailes, 'Military aspects of the war', in Warwick, op. cit., note 60, p. 65.
64 Jean de Block, 'Some lessons of the Transvaal War', *Contemporary Review*, 77, April 1900, p. 461.
65 *DE*, p. 463.
66 J. Ralph, *War's Brighter Side*, 1901, pp. 106 and 111.
67 *DE*, pp. 477–8.
68 This poem can be found in any good anthology of First World War poetry, e.g. I. Parsons (ed.), *Men Who March Away*, 1965, pp. 75.
69 W. Masson, 'Tommy Atkins in South Africa', see Warwick, op. cit., note 60, p. 123.
70 *DE*, pp. 461–3.
71 *DE*, pp. 485–6.
72 *DE*, p. 485; Pressense, op. cit., note 47, p. 158.
73 *DE*, pp. 308–310.
74 *DE*, p. 321.
75 *DE*, pp. 305–307, 321–2.
76 *DE*, p. 321.
77 *DE*, p. 306.
78 *DE*, p. 304.
79 *DE*, pp. 308–310.
80 *DE*, pp. 308–310.
81 Wilson, op. cit., note 9, p. 239.
82 Carrington, op. cit., note 8, p. 382.
83 *DE*, pp. 301–304.
84 'The Return', *DE*, p. 485.
85 'The Wage-Slaves', *DE*, p. 308.
86 'The Islanders', *DE*, pp. 301–304.
87 G.K. Chesterton, 'On Mr Kipling and making the world small', in *Heretics*, 1905, pp. 38–53.
88 Henry Austen, 'The Kipling hysteria', *Dial*, 16, 26 May 1899, pp. 327–8; see also Price, op. cit., note 49, p. 5 and Chs 3 and 4.
89 Dowden, in Green, op. cit., note 2, p. 259.
90 *Punch*, 15 January 1902, p. 52.
91 A. Waugh, 'Mr Kipling as poet: An estimate suggested by his new volume *The Five Nations*', *Book Monthly*, 1, November 1903, p. 91.
92 Ibid.
93 A. Waugh, 'The poetry of the South African campaign', *Anglo-Saxon Review*, VII, December 1900, pp. 48–9.
94 R. Buchanan, 'The voice of the hooligan', *Contemporary Review*, LXXVI, December 1899, pp. 774–89; see also Green, op. cit., note 2, p. 242 and Chapter 3, this volume, pp. 76–8.
95 M. Thompson, 'The new poetry', *Independent*, 51, 2 March 1899, p. 608.
96 Dowden, in Green, op. cit., note 2, p. 259; H.W. Laneir, 'Mr Kipling's cynical jingoism', *Dial*, 26, 16 June 1899, p. 389.

97 G. Geneung, 'An apocalypse of Kipling', *Independent*, 51, 30 March 1899, p. 888; Austen, op. cit., note 88, p. 327; Thompson, op. cit., note 95, p. 608.

Chapter 5: 'The Endless Night Begins'

1 T.S. Eliot, 'Kipling Redivivus', *Athenaeum*, May 1919, pp. 297–8.
2 Ibid., p. 297.
3 Ibid., p. 297.
4 Edward Thomas, 'The Glory', in *Collected Poems*, 1969, p. 14.
5 Ibid., 'Adlestrop', p. 66.
6 The phrase is John Morley's, the Liberal Minister and Gladstonian who was for 15 years editor of the *Fortnightly Review*, quoted in T. Shattock and M. Wolff (eds), *The Victorian Periodical Press: Samplings and Soundings*, 1982, p. 5.
7 Eliot, op. cit., note 1, p. 297.
8 Ibid., p. 298.
9 *DE*, p. 179.
10 *DE*, p. 317.
11 *DE*, p. 179.
12 *DE*, pp. 217, 216, 369 and 98 respectively.
13 'The Bridegroom', *DE*, p. 392.
14 The category of the 'people' is defined here in the manner of John Fiske in *Understanding Popular Culture*, 1989, p. 24, as a 'shifting set of allegiances that cross all social categories . . . which are described better in terms of their felt collectivity than in terms of sociological factors such as class, gender, age, race, religion or what have you'.
15 Eliot, op. cit., note 1, p. 297.
16 See M. Cohen (ed.), *Rudyard Kipling to Rider Haggard: The Record of a Friendship*, 1965, p. 102.
17 Quoted in D. Read (ed.), *Edwardian England*, 1982, pp. 14–15.
18 Quoted by W.S. Lilly, 'The parlous state of England', *The Nineteenth Century*, XLVII, April 1900, p. 592.
19 *DE*, p. 394.
20 *DE*, p. 394.
21 *DE*, pp. 382–3.
22 *DE*, pp. 382–3.
23 This phrase was used by Joseph Chamberlain in 1883 from the Liberal benches in his attack on Lord Salisbury; see D. Judd, *Balfour and the British Empire*, 1975, p. 95.
24 *DE*, pp. 382–3.
25 *DE*, pp. 382–3.
26 *DE*, pp. 382–3.
27 Cohen, op. cit., note 16, pp. 50 and 68.
28 See W.L. Arnstein, 'Edwardian politics: Turbulent spring or Indian summer?', in Alan O'Day (ed.), *The Edwardian Age*, 1978, p. 60.

29 G.R. Searle, 'Critics of Edwardian society: The case of the Radical Right', in O'Day, op. cit., note 28, p. 89.
30 Ibid., p. 83.
31 R. Rhodes James, *The British Revolution: British Politics 1880–1939*, 1978, p. 231.
32 *DE*, p. 210.
33 *DE*, p. 211.
34 *DE*, p. 211.
35 *DE*, p. 211.
36 *DE*, p. 211.
37 *DE*, p. 211.
38 *DE*, pp. 224–5.
39 *DE*, p. 225.
40 *DE*, p. 225.
41 *DE*, p. 225.
42 This story is to be found in *Traffics and Discoveries*, 1904.
43 'The Pro-Consuls', *DE*, p. 108.
44 *DE*, p. 108.
45 *DE*, p. 108.
46 *DE*, p. 282; the editorial from *The Times* is quoted in A.J.A. Morris, *The Scaremongers: The Advocacy of War and Re-armament 1890–1914*, 1984, pp. 53–4.
47 Ibid., p. 282.
48 Morris, op. cit., note 46, pp. 53–4.
49 R. Kipling and C.R.L. Fletcher, 'The Dutch in the Medway', in *A School History of England*, 1911, p. 168.
50 See D. James, *Lord Roberts*, 1941, p. 418; this speech was made on 9 November 1905.
51 Ibid., p. 453, 21 January 1912.
52 *DE*, p. 204.
53 'City of Brass', *DE*, p. 318.
54 Quoted in Rhodes James, op. cit., note 31, p. 242.
55 Ibid., p. 242.
56 Quoted in R. Scally, *The Origins of the Lord George Coalition*, 1975, pp. 188–9.
57 *DE*, pp. 315–17.
58 *DE*, pp. 315–17.
59 *DE*, pp. 315–17.
60 *DE*, pp. 315–17.
61 Quoted in Rhodes James, op. cit., note 31, p. 235. The other quotations are from 'City of Brass', *DE*, p. 318.
62 'The Female of the Species', *DE*, pp. 367–9.
63 See M. Blanch, 'Imperialism, nationalism and organized youth', in J. Clarke, C. Critcher and R. Johnson (eds), *Working Class Culture*, 1979, pp. 103–120.
64 Ibid., p. 367.
65 Ibid., p. 368.

66 *DE* p. 232.
67 *DE*, p. 232.
68 Quoted in Rhodes James, op. cit., note 31, p. 269.
69 Ibid.
70 *DE*, p. 320.
71 *DE*, p. 320.
72 See R. Wilson, 'Imperialism in crisis', in M. Langan and B. Schwarz (eds), *Crises in the British State 1880–1930*, 1985, p. 156.
73 Ibid.
74 *DE*, pp. 393, 327, 142 and 286 respectively.
75 *DE*, p. 322.
76 *DE*, p. 310.
77 J. Silkin, *Out of Battle*, 1978, p. 63.
78 Kipling, *A Book of Words*, 1928, pp. 215–16.
79 See, for example, Sorley's 'Sonnet to Germany'.
80 Kipling was active throughout the war years promoting England's 'cause'. For example, in 1915, he made a speech entitled 'Call to a Nation', which was reported in *The Times* and the *New York Times*. It was then printed by the *Daily Express* and sold at a halfpenny per copy. Few writers, before or since, have been able to command such a wide readership across the social spectrum. For many more instances of this kind, see J. McG. Stewart, *Rudyard Kipling: A Biographical Catalogue* (ed. A. Yeats), 1959. The quotation is from Trevor Wilson, *The Myriad Faces of War*, 1986, p. 731.
81 B. Bergonzi, *Heroes' Twilight*, 2nd edn, 1980; 'For All We Have & Are', *DE*, pp. 329–30.
82 J.M. Bourne, *Britain and the Great War*, 1989, p. 199.
83 *DE*, pp. 329–30.
84 *DE*, pp. 329–30.
85 *DE*, pp. 329–30.
86 The lines are from Owen's poem 'Exposure', in *Collected Poems* (ed. C. Day Lewis), 1963.
87 Ibid., the phrase is from the preface Owen wrote for his poems.
88 See 'They' and 'The General' by Siegfreid Sassoon; 'Insensibility', in Owen, op. cit., note 86; and 'Mesopotamia', *DE*, p. 300.
89 H. Brown, *Rudyard Kipling: A New Appreciation*, 1945, p. 184.
90 *DE*, p. 300.
91 These lines are from Herbert Read's poem 'To a Conscript, 1940'.
92 *DE*, p. 301.
93 *DE*, pp. 217 and 216 respectively.
94 *DE*, p. 216.
95 *DE*, p. 217.
96 *DE*, p. 217.
97 The same preoccupation with the younger generation is to be found in a poem attached to the story 'The honours of war', in *A Diversity of Creatures*, 1917. It is simply called 'The Children'; see *DE*, p. 522.
98 *DE*, p. 217.

99 *DE*, p. 216.
100 *DE*, p. 98.
101 Owen, op. cit., note 86.
102 *DE*, p. 386.
103 *DE*, p. 386.
104 'A Dead Statesman', *DE*, p. 390.
105 'Common Form', *DE*, p. 390.
106 Kipling, 'England & the English', in *A Book of Words*, 1928, p. 182.
107 The phrase is Wilfred Owen's from the preface to his poems, op. cit., note 86. Bourne provides this as the latest accurate estimate of the British dead.

Conclusion: 'A Good Bad Poet'

1 Throughout the 1920s and 1930s, Kipling had poems published in major newspapers and journals in Britain and the USA. For more information, see J. McG. Stewart, *Kipling: A Bibliographical Catalogue* (ed. A. Yeats), 1959, and the entries on the various *Inclusive Editions*.
2 This information is referred to by Vernon Scannell in *Not Without Glory: Poets of the Second World War*, 1976, pp. 7–8.
3 There were an enormous number of selections from Kipling's verse published – birthday books and scout manuals as well as the more usual kinds of anthologies.
4 *DE*, pp. 299–307.
5 'Miscellaneous Verse', *DE*, pp. 791–827.
6 The quotation from Kipling is from 'Memories', *DE*, p. 821; Disraeli's words are quoted by the obituarist of Kipling in the *Times Literary Supplement*, 25 January 1936 and the piece is reprinted in R.L. Green, *Kipling: The Critical Heritage*, 1971, p. 390.
7 'The Storm Cone', *DE*, p. 824.
8 Green, op. cit., note 6, pp. 384–92.
9 George Orwell, 'Rudyard Kipling', reprinted in E. Gilbert, *Kipling and the Critics*, 1975, pp. 74–88.
10 Ibid., pp. 74 and 84.
11 Ibid., p. 84.
12 Ibid., pp. 84 and 87.
13 Ibid., pp. 87 and 80 respectively.
14 These adjectives are used on p. 84 of Orwell's essay, op. cit., note 9.
15 Op. cit., note 9, p. 85.
16 H. Orel, 'Rudyard Kipling and the Establishment: A humanistic dilemma', *South Atlantic Quarterly*, LXXXI, 1982, p. 162.
17 Tony Harrison, *V and Other Poems*, 1990.
18 Tony Harrison quoted in N. Astley (ed.), *Tony Harrison*, 1991, p. 9.
19 The description 'good bad poet' is used on p. 84 of Orwell's essay, op. cit., note 9. The other quotations are taken from pp. 86, 85 and 86 respectively.

Bibliography

NB As has been indicated in the Notes, many of the reviews referred to in the text are to be found in R.L. Green's *Kipling: The Critical Heritage* (1971). Where this is the case, they have not been listed separately.

Adams, F. (1893) 'Mr Kipling's verse', *Fortnightly Review*, 60 (OS), November.

Amis, K. (1975) *Rudyard Kipling and His World*. London: Thames & Hudson.

Anderson, P. (1983) *Imagined Communities*. London: Verso.

Arnstein, W.L. (1978) 'Edwardian politics: turbulent spring or Indian summer?' In A.O. O'Day (ed.) *The Edwardian Age*. London: Macmillan.

Astley, N. (1991) *Tony Harrison*. Newcastle upon Tyne: Bloodaxe Books Ltd.

Attridge, D., Bennington, G. and Young, R. (1988) *Post-Structuralism and the Question of History*. Cambridge: Cambridge University Press.

Auden, W.H. (1943) 'The poet of the encirclement', *The New Republic*, 25 October.

Austen, H. (1899) 'The Kipling hysteria', *Dial*, 16, 26 May.

Bailey, P. (1986) *Music-Hall – The Business of Pleasure*. Milton Keynes: Open University Press.

Ballhatchet, K. (1982) *Race, Sex and Class under the Raj*. London: Weidenfeld & Nicholson.

Bennett, T. (1988) 'Texts in history: the determinations of readings and their texts'. In D. Attridge, G. Bennington and R. Young (eds) *Post-Structuralism and the Question of History*. Cambridge: Cambridge University Press.

Bennett, T., Martin, G. and Mercer, C. (1981) *Culture, Ideology and Social Process*. Milton Keynes: Open University Press.

Bennett, T., Mercer, C. and Woollacott, J. (1986) *Popular Culture and Social Process*. Milton Keynes: Open University Press.

Benson, A.C. (1899) *Life of Edward White Benson Sometime Archbishop of Canterbury*. London: John Murray.

Bergonzi, B. (1980). *Heroes' Twilight*. London: Macmillan, 2nd edn.
Besant, W. (1897) *The Rise of Empire*. London: Marshall.
Besant, W. (1900) 'Is it the voice of the hooligan?', *Contemporary Review*, LXXVII.
Bhaba, H. (1990) *Nation and Narration*. London: Routledge.
Birkenhead, Lord (1978) *Rudyard Kipling*. New York: Random House.
Bivona, D. (1990) *Desire and Contradiction: Imperial Divisions and Domestic Debates in Victorian Literature*. Manchester: Manchester University Press.
Blanche, M. (1980) 'British society and the War'. In P. Warwick (ed.) *The South African War: The Anglo-Boer War 1899–1902*. Harlow: Longmans.
Block, J. de (1900) 'Some lessons of the Transvaal War', *Contemporary Review*, 77, April.
Bodelsen, C. (1964) *Aspects of Kipling's Art*. Manchester: Manchester University Press.
Bond, B. (1961) 'The late Victorian army', *History Today*, XI.
Booth, J.B. (1925) *Old Pink 'Un Days*. New York: Dodd, Mead.
Booth, J.B. (1943) *The Days We Knew*. London: T. Werner, Laurie.
Bourne, J.M. (1989) *Britain and the Great War*. London: Routledge.
Bowie, M. (1987) *Freud, Proust and Lacan: Theory as Fiction*. Cambridge: Cambridge University Press.
Boyd, C.W. (ed.) (1914) *Mr Chamberlain's Speeches*, Vols 1 and 2. London: Constable.
Brantlinger, P. (1988) *Rule of Darkness: British Literature and Imperialism*. London: Cornell University Press.
Bratton, J.S. (1975) *The Victorian Popular Ballad*. London: Macmillan.
Bratton, J.S. (1978) *Kipling's Magic Art*, The British Academy, Vol LXIV. Oxford: Oxford University Press.
Bratton, J.S. (1986) *Music-Hall: Performance and Style*. Milton Keynes: Open University Press.
Brown, H. (1945) *Rudyard Kipling: A New Appreciation*. London: Hamish Hamilton.
Browne, H. (1974) *Joseph Chamberlain – Radical Imperialist*. London: Longman.
Buchanan, R. (1899) 'The voice of the hooligan', *Contemporary Review*, Vol LXXVI, December.
Carrington, C. (1978) *Rudyard Kipling: His Life and Work*. Harmondsworth: Penguin, 3rd edn revised.
Chesterton, G.K. (1905) *Heretics*. London: Bodley Head.
Clarke, J., Critcher, C. and Johnson, R. (1979) *Working Class Culture*. London: Hutchinson.
Cohen, M. (1965) *Rudyard Kipling to Rider Haggard: The Record of a Friendship*. London: Hutchinson.
Colls, R. and Dodd, P. (1986) *Englishness: Politics and Culture 1880–1920*. London: Croom Helm.
Cornell, L. (1966) *Kipling in India*. London: Macmillan.
Couch, A. Quiller. (1898) 'Reviews and reminders: on some living English poets', *English Illustrated Magazine*, Vol. X, 120, September.

Crankshaw, E. (1952) *The Forsaken Idea*. London: Longmans, Green & Co.
Critcher, C. and Crossick, G. (1977) *The Lower Middle-Class in Britain 1870–1914*. London: Croom Helm.
Cunningham, H. (1981) 'The language of patriotism 1750–1914', *History Workshop Journal*, 12, Autumn.
Dicey, E. (1877) 'Mr Gladstone and our empire', *The Nineteenth Century*, 11, September.
Dobree, R. (1967) *Rudyard Kipling: Realist and Fabulist*. Oxford: Oxford University Press.
Donald, J. (1988) 'How English is it?', *New Formations*, No. 6, Winter.
Dowden, E. (1901) 'The poetry of Mr Kipling', *New Liberal Review*, Vol. XXVIII, February.
Eagleton, T. (1981) *Walter Benjamin*. London: Verso.
Eby, C. (1988) *The Road to Armageddon: The Martial Spirit in English Literature 1830–1914*. Durham, NC: Duke University Press.
Edwardes, M. (1988) *The Sahibs and The Lotus*. London: Constable.
Eldridge, C. (1973) *England's Mission: The Imperial Idea in the Age of Gladstone and Disraeli 1868–1880*. London: Macmillan.
Eldridge, C. (1978) *Victorian Imperialism*. London: Hodder & Stoughton.
Eldridge, C. (ed.) (1984) *British Imperialism in the Nineteenth Century*. London: Macmillan.
Eliot, T.S. (1919) 'Kipling Redivivus', *The Athenaeum*, May.
Eliot, T.S. (1941) *A Choice of Kipling's Verse*. London: Faber & Faber, 6th edn.
Faber, R. (1966) *The Vision and the Need: Late Victorian Imperialist Aims*. London: Faber & Faber.
Fido, M. (1974) *Rudyard Kipling*. London: Hamlyn.
Field, H.J. (1982) *Toward a Programme of Imperial Life: The British Empire at the Turn of the Century*. Chicago: Greenwood Press.
Fiske, J. (1989) *Understanding Popular Culture*. London: Unwin Hyman.
Forster, H.O. Arnold (1904) *The Citizen Reader: For the Use of Schools*. London: Cassells.
Galbraith, J.S. (1952) 'The pamphlet campaign on the Boer War', *Journal of Modern History*, XXIV, No. 2, June.
Garvin, J. (1934) *The Life of Joseph Chamberlain, Vol. 3: 1895–1900. Empire and World Policy*. London: Macmillan.
Geneung, G. (1899) 'An apocalypse of Kipling', *Independent*, 30 March.
Gilbert, E. (1966) *Kipling and The Critics*. London: Peter Owen.
Gilbert, E. (1972) *The Good Kipling: Studies in the Short Story*. Manchester: Manchester University Press.
Gladstone, W.E. (1877) 'Aggression on Egypt and Freedom in the East', *The Nineteenth Century*, 11, August.
Gollin, A.M. (1964) *Pro-Consul in Politics*. London: Anthony Blond.
Gooch, G.P. (1901) *Imperialism*. Oxford: Oxford University Press.
Gramsci, A. (1971) *Selections from the Prison Notebooks*. London: Lawrence & Wishart.
Green, M. (1980) *Dreams of Adventure. Deeds of Empire*. New York: Basic Books.

Green, R.L. (1971) *Kipling: The Critical Heritage*. London: Routledge & Kegan Paul.
Gross, J. (ed.) (1975) *Rudyard Kipling: The Man, his Work and his World*. London: Weidenfeld & Nicholson.
Harrison, F. (1894) 'The evolution of our race: a reply', *Fortnightly Review*, 60.
Harrison, T. (1987) *Selected Poems*. London: Penguin, 2nd edn.
Henley, W.E. (1900) 'Concerning Atkins', *Pall Mal! Magazine*, XXI.
Henn, T.R. (1967) *Kipling*. Edinburgh: Oliver & Boyd.
Heyck, T.W. (1982) *The Transformation of Intellectual Life in Victorian England*. London: Croom Helm.
Hobson, J. (1901) *The Psychology of Jingoism*. London: Grant Richards.
Howard, D. (1970) *London Theatres and Music Halls 1850–1950*. London: The Library Association.
Hunter, W.W. (1888) 'Departmental Ditties & Other Verses', *The Academy*, Vol. 3, No. 852, 1 September.
Hunter, W. (1889) 'Review of soldiers three', *The Spectator*, 23 March.
Humphries, S. (1981) *Hooligans or Rebels?* Oxford: Blackwell.
Hutchins, F. (1967) *The Illusion of Permanence: British Imperialism in India*. New Jersey: Princeton University Press.
Hyam, R. (1976) *Britain's Imperial Century*. London: Batsford.
Ionescu, G. and Gellner, E. (1969) *Populism: Its Meaning and National Character*. London: Macmillan.
Islam, S. (1975) *Kipling's Law*. London: Macmillan.
James, D. (1941) *Lord Roberts*. London: Hollis & Carter.
Jones, K. (1919) *Fleet St and Downing St*. London: Hutchinson.
Judd, D. (1975) *Balfour and the British Empire*. London: Macmillan.
Keating, P.J. (1971) *The Working-Classes in Victorian Fiction*. London: Routledge & Kegan Paul.
Kincaid, D. (1938) *British Social Life in India 1608–1937*. London: Routledge & Kegan Paul.
Kipling, R. (1982) *The Definitive Edition of Rudyard Kipling's Verse*. London: Hodder & Stoughton.
Kipling, R. (1989). *Barrack-Room Ballads & Other Verses*. London: Methuen.
Kipling, R. (1986) *Early Verse by Rudyard Kipling 1879–89. Unpublished, Uncollected and Rarely Collected Poems* (ed.) A. Rutherford. Oxford: Oxford University Press.
Kipling, R. (1904) *Many Inventions*. London: Macmillan.
Kipling, R. (1990) *War Stories and Poems*. Oxford: Oxford University Press.
Kipling, R. and Fletcher, C.R.L. (1911) *A School History of England*. Oxford: Clarendon Press.
Kipling, R. (1894) 'My first book', *McClure's Magazine* 3, No. 6, November.
Kipling, R. (1917) *A Diversity of Creatures*. London: Macmillan.
Kipling, R. (1907) *Abaft the Funnel*. New York: Doubleday Page & Co.
Kipling, R. (1989) *Kim*. London: Penguin.
Kipling, R. (1987) *Plain Tales from the Hills*. London: Penguin.
Kipling, R. (1987) *Rewards and Fairies*. London: Penguin.
Kipling, R. (1909) *Soldiers Three*. London: Macmillan.

Kipling, R. (1981) *Something of Myself*. London: Penguin.
Kipling, R. (1987) *Stalky and Co*. London: Penguin.
Kipling, R. (1982) *The Day's Work*. London: Macmillan.
Kipling, R. (1988) *The Light that Failed*. London: Penguin.
Kipling, R. (1904) *Traffics and Discoveries*. London: Macmillan.
Kipling, R. (1928) *A Book of Words*. London: Macmillan.
Koebner, R. and Schmidt, H. Dan. (1964) *Imperialism: The Story and Significance of a Political Word 1840–1960*. Cambridge: Cambridge University Press.
Koss, S. (1973) *Pro-Boers*. Chicago: Chicago University Press.
Koss, S. (1990) *The Rise and Fall Of the Political Press in Britain*. London: Fontana.
Laneir, H.W. (1899) 'Mr Kipling's cynical jingoism', *Dial*, 26, 16 June.
Lang, A. (1888) 'Review of *Departmental Ditties*', *The Academy*, 3, No. 852, September.
Langan, M. and Schwarz, B. (1985) *Crises in the British State 1880–1930*. London: Hutchinson.
Le Gallienne, R. (1900) *Rudyard Kipling: A Criticism*. London: John Lane.
Lilly, W.S. (1900) 'The parlous state of England', *The Nineteenth Century*, Vol. XLVII, April.
McKenzie, J.M. (1984) *Propaganda and Empire*. Manchester: Manchester University Press.
McKenzie, J.M. (1986) *Imperialism and Popular Culture*. Manchester: Manchester University Press.
Magnus, P. (1954) *Gladstone: A Biography*. London: John Murray.
Mannoni, A. (1989) *Prospero and Caliban*. London: Routledge.
Mannsaker, F. (1980) 'Anglo-Indian racial attitudes', *Victorian Studies*, 24, No. 1.
Marshall, H.R. (1899) 'Kipling and the racial instinct', *Century*, 58, 3, July.
Martin, B. Jr (1969) *New India 1885: British Official Policy and the Emergence of the Indian National Congress*. Oxford: Oxford University.
Mason, P. (1975) *Kipling: The Glass, the Shadow and the Fire*. London: Cape.
Maurice, A.B. (1899) 'Kipling's verse people', *The Bookman*, Vol. 9, March.
Memmi, A. (1965) *The Colonizer and the Colonized*. New York: The Orion Press.
Meyers, J. (1972) *Fiction and the Colonial Experience*. Ipswich: Boydell Press.
Milner, A. (1913) *The Nation and the Empire*. London: Constable & Co.
Moore, R.J. (1966) *Liberalism and Indian Politics 1872–1922*. London: Edward Arnold.
Moore-Gilbert, B. (1986) *Kipling and 'Orientalism'*. London: Croom Helm.
Morris, A.J. (1984) *The Scaremongers: The Advocacy of War and Re-Armament 1890–1914*. London: Routledge & Kegan Paul.
Morris, J. (1979) *Farewell the Trumpets: An Imperial Retreat*. Harmondsworth: Penguin.
Nandy, A. (1981) *The Intimate Enemy – Loss and Recovery of the Self Under Colonialism*. New Delhi: Oxford University Press.
Norton, C.E. (1897) 'Kipling's poetry', *Atlantic Monthly*, Vol. LXXIX, January.
Oaten, E.F. (1908) *A Sketch of Anglo-Indian Literature*. London: Kegan Paul Trench Trubner & Co Ltd.

O'Day, A. (ed.) (1978) *The Edwardian Age*. London: Macmillan.

Orel, H. (1982) 'Rudyard Kipling and the establishment: a humanistic dilemma', *South Atlantic Quarterly*, LXXXI.

Orel, H. (ed.) (1989) *Critical Essays on Rudyard Kipling*. Boston: G.K. Hall & Co.

Orel, H. (1990) *A Kipling Chronology*. London: Macmillan.

Owen, W. (1963) *Collected Poems* (ed.) C. Day Lewis. London: Chatto & Windus.

Page, N. (1984) *A Kipling Companion*. London: Macmillan.

Parry, A. (1985) 'Reading formations in the Victorian periodical press: the reception of Kipling 1888–1891', *Literature and History*, Vol. 11, 2, Autumn.

Parry, B. (1972) *Delusions and Discoveries*. London: Penguin.

Parry, B. (1987) 'Problems in current theories of colonial discourse', *Oxford Literary Review*, 9, 1/2.

Parry, B. (1988) 'The content and discontents of Kipling's imperialism', *New Formations*, No. 6, Winter.

Parsons, I. (1965) *Men Who March Away*. London: Chatto & Windus.

Philips, C. (ed.) (1962) *The Evolution of India and Pakistan 1858–1947: Select Documents*. London: Allen & Unwin.

Phillips, G. (1979) *The Diehards: Aristocratic Society and Politics in Edwardian England*. Harvard: Harvard University Press.

Pinney, T. (ed.) (1990) *The Letters of Rudyard Kipling, Vols 1 and 2*. London: Macmillan.

Porter, A. (1980) *The Origins of the South African War*. London: Croom Helm.

Porter, B. (1983) *Britain, Europe and the World 1850–1982*. London: Allen & Unwin.

Porter, B. (1984) *The Lion's Share*. New York: Longman, 2nd edn.

Presense, F. (1899) *Contemporary Review*, LXXV, February.

Price, R. (1972) *An Imperial War and the British Working-Class*. London: Routledge.

Price, R. (1977) 'Society, status and jingoism: the social roots of lower middle-class patriotism 1870–1900'. In G. Crossick (ed.) *The Lower Middle-Class in Britain 1870–1914–1977*. London: Croom Helm.

Ralph, J. (1901) *War's Brighter Side*. London: C. Arthur Pearson.

Read, D. (ed.) (1982) *Edwardian England*. London: Croom Helm.

Rhodes James, R. (1978) *The British Revolution: British Politics 1880–1939*. London: Methuen.

Ritchie, J. Ewing (1880) *Days and Nights in London*. London: Tinsley Brothers.

Robbins, K. (1990) 'National identity and history: past, present and future', *History*, Autumn.

Roberts, R. (1971) *The Classic Slum*. Manchester: Manchester University Press.

Robertson, J. McKinnon (1901) *Wrecking the Empire*. London: Grant Richards.

Rosebery, Lord (1900) *Questions of Empire*. London: Arthur L. Humphreys.

Rutherford, A. (ed.) (1964) *Kipling's Mind and Art*. London: Oliver & Boyd.

Said, E. (1978) *Orientalism*. London: Penguin.

Said, E. (1988) *Nationalism, Colonialism and Literature: Yeats and Decolonisation*, Field Day Pamphlet No. 15. Derry: Field Day Theatre Co. Ltd.

Samuel, R. (ed.) (1989) *Patriotism: The Making and Unmaking of British National Identity*, Vols 1, 2 and 3. London: Routledge.

Sandison, A. (1967) *The Wheel of Empire*. London: Macmillan.

Scally, R. (1975) *The Origins of the Lloyd George Coalition*. Princeton: Princeton University Press.

Scannell, V. (1976) *Not Without Glory: Poets of the Second World War*. London: The Woburn Press.

Searle, G. (1971) *The Quest for National Efficiency*. Oxford: Blackwell.

Searle, G. (1978) 'Critics of Edwardian society: the case of the Radical Right'. In A. O'Day (ed.) *The Edwardian Age*. London: Macmillan.

Senelick, L. (1975) 'Politics as entertainment: Victorian music-hall songs', *Victorian Studies*, Vol. XIX, December.

Shanks, E. (1970) *Rudyard Kipling: A Study in Literature and Political Ideas*. New York: Cooper Square Publishing Inc.

Shannon, R. (1976) *Crisis in British Imperialism 1865–1915*. London: Granada Publishing Ltd.

Shattock, J. and Wolff, M. (1982) *The Victorian Periodical Press: Samplings and Soundings*. Leicester: Leicester University Press.

Silkin, J. (1978) *Out of Battle*. Oxford: Oxford University Press.

Spiers, E. (1980) *The Army and Society*. Manchester: Manchester University Press.

Stallybrass, P. and White, A. (1986) *The Politics and Poetics of Transgression*. London: Routledge.

Stead, W. (1899) *Review of Reviews*, 15 April.

Steadman-Jones, G. (1983) *Languages of Class: Working-Class Culture and Working-Class Politics in London 1870–1900*. Cambridge: Cambridge University Press.

Stewart, J. Mc. G. (1959) *Rudyard Kipling: A Bibliographical Catalogue* (ed.) A.W. Yeats. Toronto: Dalhousie University Press and University of Toronto Press. Halifax, Nova Scotia.

Stokes, E. (1960) *The Political Ideas of English Imperialism*. Oxford: Oxford University Press.

Summerfield, P. (1986) 'Patriotism and empire: music-hall entertainment 1870–1914'. In J. M. McKenzie (ed.) *Imperialism and Popular Culture*. Manchester: Manchester University Press.

Summers, A. (1976) 'Militarism in Britain before the War', *History Workshop Journal*, 2, Autumn.

Sykes, A. (1983) 'The Radical Right and the crisis of Conservatism before the First World War', *Historical Journal*, Vol. 26, 3 September.

Thomas, E. (1969) *Collected Poems*. London: Faber & Faber.

Thompson, M. (1899) 'The new poetry', *Independent*, 51, 2 March.

Tompkins, J.M.S. (1959) *The Art of Rudyard Kipling*. London: Methuen.

Van Wyk Smith, J. (1975) *Drummer Hodge: The Poetry of the Anglo-Boer War 1899–1902*. Oxford: Oxford University Press.

Ward, T.H. (1887) *The Reign of Queen Victoria*. London: Smith Elder.

Warwick, P. (ed.) (1980) *The South African War: The Anglo-Boer War 1899–1902*. Harlow: Longmans.

Waugh, A. (1900) 'The poetry of the South African campaign', *Anglo-Saxon*, VII, December.

Waugh, A. (1903) 'Mr Kipling as poet: an estimate suggested by his new volume *The Five Nations*', *Book Monthly*, 1, November.

Weygandt, A. (1939) *Kipling's Reading and Its Influence on His Poetry*. Unpublished PhD thesis, US.

Williams, P. (1986) 'Colonial literature and the notion of Britishness', *Journal of Literature Teaching Politics*, 5.

Wilson, A. (1977) *The Strange Ride of Rudyard Kipling*. London: Secker & Warburg.

Wilson, R. (1985) 'Imperialism in crisis'. In M. Langan and B. Schwarz (eds) *Crises in the British State 1880–1930*. London: Hutchinson.

Wilson, T. (1986) *The Myriad Faces of War*. Cambridge: Polity Press.

Woodruff, P. (1954) *The Men Who Ruled India: The Guardians*. London: Jonathan Cape.

Wright, D. (1978) 'The Great War, propaganda and English men of letters 1914–1916', *Literature and History*, Spring.

Wurgaft, L. (1983) *The Imperial Imagination*. Middletown, Connecticut: Wesleyan University Press.

Index